THE SECRET OF FATIMA
Fact and Legend

Our Lady of Fatima

THE SECRET OF FATIMA
Fact and Legend

JOAQUIN MARIA ALONSO, C.M.F.

*Translated by the Dominican Nuns
of the Perpetual Rosary*

THE RAVENGATE PRESS
Cambridge

ISBN: 0-911218-14-9   (Clothbound)
ISBN: 0-911218-15-7   (Paperbound)

LIBRARY OF CONGRESS CATALOGING IN PUBLICATION DATA

Alonso, Joaquin Maria.
  The Secret of Fatima.

  Translation of La Verdad Sobre el Secreto de Fatima,
Fatima sin mitos.
  1. Fatima, Nossa Senhora da.   I. Title.
BT660.F3A4513   232.91   79-13182

2nd Printing, 1982

Contents

PART III: THE MEANING OF THE SECRET

Illustrations

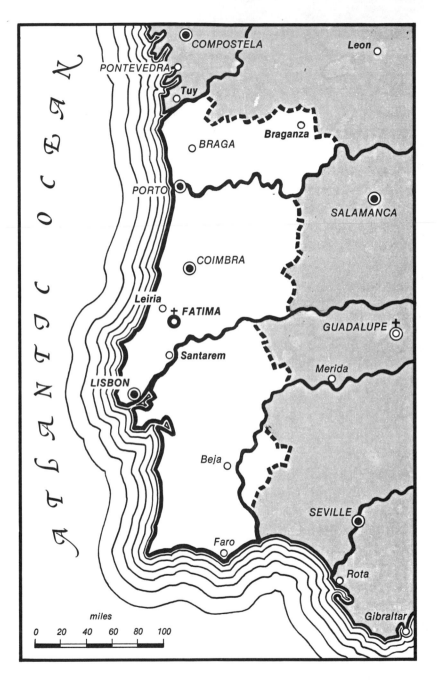

Portugal and western Spain

Introduction

IN THE YEAR 1917, AT A SPOT NOT FAR FROM THE VILLAGE
of Fatima in Portugal, the Mother of God appeared
six times in successive months to three shepherd
children. Today a magnificent basilica marks the
place of the apparitions, visited each year by hun-
dreds of thousands of pilgrims. Though the shrine is
the site of numerous miracles, it is not principally for
its "cures" that Fatima is famous. It is known, rather,
chiefly for its message: those words, so urgent and
insistent, spoken by Our Lady to the three young
children in that remote pasture. This is what has
captured the attention of the faithful since the first
reports of Fatima began to be circulated.

There is one part of the Fatima message, however,
that has never been publicly revealed. It is contained
in a sealed letter written by Lucia dos Santos, the only
surviving member of the three to whom Our Lady

appeared, now a Carmelite nun with the name Sister Mary Lucia of the Immaculate Heart. Lucia had written this letter in late 1943 or early 1944, at the insistence of her ordinary, the Bishop of Leiria. The letter was sealed, its contents known only to Lucia herself, with the instruction that it should be opened "not before 1960." At first the letter was kept in a safe at the bishopric in Leiria, but in 1947 it was removed to the Vatican.

As 1960 approached, the letter containing the Secret became an object of world-wide publicity and curiosity. Noting that previously-published parts of the Fatima message showed that Our Lady had in 1917 foretold both the end of World War I and the coming of World War II, sensation-mongers speculated freely as to what apocalyptic pronouncements the letter might contain.

And so, to a crescendo of excitement and anticipation, 1960 arrived and Lucia's letter was opened. Pope John XXIII read the letter, showed it to a few close aides, and then ordered it returned to the Vatican Archives—its contents still unrevealed.

The resulting disappointment was unquestionably due to the sensationalism that had preceded the letter's opening. Nevertheless, the sensationalists quickly went to work again, assuring the public that the Pope had not dared to publish the Secret because it was simply too terrifying. (On the other side, of course, were the detractors, who said he had not revealed it because it was just not worth revealing.) The worst effect of all this confusion was that the known parts of Our Lady's message at Fatima were being disparaged and obscured. And that message was far too clear, and too important, for such a thing to happen.

Clearly what was needed was a full, factual and objective study of the Secret of Fatima, seen in the light of the whole Fatima message, as well as the whole Catholic Faith. This need was definitively filled in 1976 with the European publication of *La Verdad Sobre el Secreto de Fatima*, by Father Joaquin Maria Alonso.

It is not surprising that this book, now published in English for the first time, was an immediate and huge success; for its author was supremely suited for his task. Founder and director of the *Centro Mariano* in Madrid, a distinguished teacher and Marian scholar, Father Alonso is widely regarded as the foremost authority on Fatima apart from Lucia herself. (When Lucia's memoirs were recently published, he was chosen to write the introduction and commentary.)

With scholarship and insight, Father Alonso traces the history of the Secret. He shows that the sensationalist literature purporting to deal with it is not only unfounded but opposed to the whole spirit and intent of Fatima. Finally, Father Alonso offers his own carefully-reasoned conclusions as to what the Secret might be. Without presuming to speak decisively on the matter, he presents inferences that are "well founded on solid reasons and historical affirmations which allow us to speak with maximum probability."

Father Alonso's conjectures as to the nature of the Secret are serious and sobering but, at the same time, charged with Christian hope. He is likewise careful to point out that Fatima must not be seen as a theological novelty, "an interpolation introduced into the deposit of Faith." It belongs to the mainstream of Catholic evangelical tradition. No one, therefore, should expect to find in the Secret "a new doctrine, something original which has come to revolutionize dogma, morals, or Christian spirituality."

It is this insistence by Father Alonso that Fatima and its Secret must always be seen in the context of revealed truth as taught by the Church that distinguishes his book from most "apocalyptic" literature and gives it enduring theological value.

Father Alonso assumes on the part of his readers a familiarity with the principal details of the Fatima story. Indeed, he insists that the Secret can be studied only in terms of the total Fatima event. The following synopsis, therefore, is not meant to be a substitute for the obligatory full account available in a number of excellent books. It is presented simply as a sort of "Fatima refresher," an aid to the reader in recalling the main episodes, places and dates referred to by Father Alonso.

1916—Lucia dos Santos, aged nine, and her two cousins, Francisco and Jacinta Marto, aged eight and six, while watching their families' sheep, see "a light...in the form of a young man." Three times during that year the apparition visits and speaks with the children. Identifying himself as the Angel of Portugal, he teaches them to pray and urges them to make sacrifices. "The hearts of Jesus and Mary have designs of mercy on you," he tells them.

May 13, 1917—Tending their sheep at the Cova da Iria, a plot of outlying pasture and farm land belonging to the Santos family, the three children suddenly behold "a Lady all dressed in white...more brilliant than the sun." The Lady tells the children not to be afraid, that she is from heaven, and asks them to return to the Cova on the same day for the next six months. She tells them she will take them to heaven (though Francisco "must say many Rosaries") and asks them, "Are you willing to offer yourselves to God to bear all the sufferings He wills to send you...?" When they answer that they are willing, the Lady tells them, "Then you are going to have much to suffer, but the grace of God will be your comfort." As she says this, the Lady spreads her hands, "communicating to us a light so intense that, as it streamed from her hands, its rays penetrated our hearts and the innermost depths of our souls." Then, urging the children to pray the Rosary daily for peace in the world and the end of the war, she departs.

June 13—Our Lady tells Lucia that she will take Jacinta and Francisco to heaven soon but Lucia herself must wait: "Jesus wishes to make use of you to make me known and loved. He wants to establish in the world devotion to my Immaculate Heart."

July 13—Our Lady shows the children a horrifying vision of hell but consoles them with the assurance that devotion to her Immaculate Heart can save sinners from going there. She tells them that the war will soon end, but that if people continue to offend God, "a worse one will break out during the pontificate of Pius XI." To punish the world for its sins, God will permit "war, famine, and persecutions of the Church and the Holy Father." To prevent these catastrophies, Our Lady promises to return "to ask for the consecration of Russia to my Immaculate Heart, and the Communion of Reparation on the First Saturdays. If my requests are heeded, Russia will be converted, and there will be peace; if not, she will spread her errors throughout the world, causing wars and persecutions of the Church." (*Note:* The above revelations will not be made known by Lucia until 1941, in her third Memoir. They form the first two parts of the Secret of Fatima. The third part is the subject of this book.)

August 19—By this time, word of the apparitions has gotten out and crowds are beginning to gather at the Cova da Iria on the thirteenth of each month. To put an end to this "invasion of mysticism," the local magistrate, a freethinker and anti-Catholic, orders the children taken into custody. He then tries to frighten them into declaring the apparitions a hoax or, at least, to make them promise they will not return to the Cova da Iria. He does not succeed, but does prevent their being at the Cova on the thirteenth of this month. On the following Sunday after Mass, the children visit the Cova to say their Rosary, and in a place not far away, called Valinhos, Our Lady appears to them. In answer to Lucia's request, she promises them that at the last apparition, in October, she will perform a great miracle, so that all may see and believe.

September 13—Our Lady tells the children to continue to pray the Rosary for peace and repeats her promise of great wonders at the next apparition.

October 13—The roads leading to Fatima are so crowded the children can scarcely move through the throngs. At the Cova the eventual crowd is estimated at more than 100,000 people. When Our Lady appears, she asks that a chapel be built there in her honor. Then she performs the promised miracle: a stupendous, riveting display in which the sun seems to "dance" in the sky, whirling about and changing colors like a giant fiery pinwheel. The wonder lasts for about ten minutes and is seen not only at the Cova but over the whole area, by believers and unbelievers alike. Finally Our Lady re-appears to the children, together with Saint Joseph and the Child Jesus.

Though these six appearances constitute the Apparitions of Our Lady of Fatima in the strict sense, they were not the last time the three children would be visited by Our Lady. She would appear to both Francisco and Jacinta before their deaths, his in 1919, hers in 1920. And Lucia would be favored with a number of apparitions by Our Lady and also by her Divine Son.

Especially important are the apparitions of December 10, 1925 and June 13, 1929. The former occurred at Pontevedra, the latter at Tuy, both towns just north of Portugal in Spain, at convents of the Sisters of Saint Dorothy, a community that Lucia entered in 1925 and where she remained until 1948, when she joined the Carmelites at Coimbra, in Portugal. These two apparitions fulfilled the promise of Our Lady on July 13, 1917 that she would return with special requests. In 1925 she appeared with the Child Jesus, and after showing her heart surrounded by thorns, told Lucia to "announce that I promise to assist at the hour of death with all the graces necessary for salvation, all those who, for five successive months on the first Saturday, confess, receive Holy Communion, recite the Rosary and keep me company for fifteen minutes while meditating on the mysteries of the Rosary in a spirit of reparation."

In the 1929 apparition, Our Lady told Lucia, "God asks the Holy Father, in union with all the bishops of the world, to make the consecration of Russia to my Immaculate Heart, promising to save it by this means."

This, in brief, is the background against which Father Alonso presents his study. It is a work which must, in the absence of any direct knowledge of the contents of Lucia's letter, stand as a central part of the Fatima literature. For it not only provides great insight into the nature of the much-disputed Secret, but in doing so recalls and reemphasizes the primary, abiding message of Our Lady of Fatima.

This English translation of the original Spanish text is by the Dominican Nuns of the Perpetual Rosary, an English-speaking community residing at the Monastery of Pius XII in Fatima.

Prologue

ALTHOUGH THIS BOOK MAY BE CLASSIFIED AS "POPULAR,"
it is a serious study. Every assertion—or correction of
previous error—is well-founded, whether it be in the
realm of history, historical criticism or theology.
Since, however, this book is meant for the average
reader, I did not wish to overload it with footnotes. A
major work now being published in Portuguese
contains not only a critical edition of the texts but
also critical studies of all the questions raised by the
event and message of Fatima. What is offered here is
as it were the essence distilled from that more
extensive work.

My primary intention is twofold. I want first to do
away once and for all with the mystifications, the
caricatures, the hair-raising exaggerations, the cheap
and sensational apocalyptic writings which have been
produced on the subject of Fatima and its Secret. To

achieve this first end, there was only one way to proceed: to tell the truth and nothing but the truth.

But the truth about the Secret of Fatima contains certain highly dramatic aspects. Although in no way meant to fill us with fear and dread, Fatima and its Secret do present us with something deeply serious since they bring us face to face with the mysteries of eternal life.

Finally, I would like to point out that since this book deals particularly with the Secret of Fatima, it does not attempt to give a synopsis either of the story of Fatima or of its wonderful message. The reader would do well, therefore, to preface his reading of this work by acquainting himself with the events and the Message in general, which are to be found in innumerable books.

May the Lord bring us, by means of Our Lady of Fatima, to the perfection of the love of Jesus Christ, through the Holy Spirit.

Joaquin Maria Alonso, C.M.F.
July 13, 1976

PART I

Facts and Texts
Concerning
The Secret of Fatima

The first Bishop of Leiria, the late Dom Jose Correia da Silva, holding the letter containing the Secret

1

The Original Secret

WHEN PEOPLE SPEAK OF THE SECRET OF FATIMA, THEY are using an ambiguous phrase which has been the source of much confusion. The expression can only be understood correctly in terms of what happened at Fatima. There was a certain holding back, an attitude of reserve, about some things, and the children, obeying a prohibition from Heaven itself, revealed them only with utmost caution. Finally, the ecclesiastical authorities responsible for disclosing these supernatural occurrences contributed to the development of the atmosphere of secrecy by the very prudence with which they made them known. This extreme caution has also provoked the often well justified criticism of theologians.

Fatima today has very little secret still undivulged. The facts and the texts, however, can bring us light and good judgment with regard to it, and this is what we shall endeavor to obtain in Part One.

The earliest extraordinary happenings at Fatima began in the year 1915 with strange occurrences in which Lucia and some young girls (neither Jacinta nor Francisco were present) saw a strange figure which appeared to them several times. The other young girls made these events known, but Lucia only spoke of them when obliged to do so by her mother's probing questions. What she had to suffer on that account led Lucia to adopt an attitude of natural reserve, which events of a higher order later confirmed.

Lucia recommended silence to her cousins Francisco and Jacinta on the occasion of the apparitions of the Angel in 1916. However, as she herself put it later, this was not necessary, for "the very Apparition itself imposed secrecy. It was so intimate that it was not easy to speak of it at all."

In fact, the apparitions of the Angel remained a secret, known to very few, until May of 1942, when the Cardinal of Lisbon made them public in a conspicuous manner. Lucia was in no way at fault in this, for as early as 1917 she had been prohibited by her directors from speaking of these apparitions, in order that Our Lady's message might be more readily accepted.

After Our Lady's first appearance in May, 1917, the children agreed, to avoid annoyances, that they would keep silence about certain details. These were two: the promise they had received that they would go to heaven, and the reference to reparation to the Heart of Mary, already revealed to them in this first apparition. Our Lady had not ordered them to keep silence about either of these two things. Nevertheless, by a kind of heavenly instinct, the children understood that they should say nothing of them. After the apparitions of June and July, the little seers—and later Lucia, the only one surviving— were even more determined not to speak of reparation to the Heart of Mary, for this was so closely connected with the real Secret which they had received that to mention it at all would have led to the revelation of what they had specifically been told not to disclose.

Of what avail, however, were the children's good intentions in the face of little Jacinta's passionate enthusiasm and the providential plan of God to make the apparitions known? On that same glorious afternoon of Sunday, May 13, the very first thing Jacinta said when she saw her mother was, "Oh, mother, I saw Our Lady!" And not only that but, unable to contain herself, she revealed also that Our Lady had promised to take them to heaven.

"But what did you say?" asked Lucia reproachfully. "I said," answered Jacinta, "that this Lady promised to take us to heaven." "To think you told them that!" replied Lucia. And Jacinta, in tears, went on, "Forgive me. I won't tell anybody anything ever again!" Indeed, after that, if anyone was excessively brief in her declarations, it was Jacinta.

Here we see what could well have been one of the secrets of Fatima. This "personal" secret of the little shepherds, safely assured to going to heaven, and quite soon, was in fact revealed on the very day of the first apparition. For Francisco and Jacinta, who died in 1919 and 1920 respectively, that secret is already a wonderful and luminous reality. For Lucia, what must it be like to go on living in the obscurity of faith, while having at the same time a certain hope of salvation?

In the apparition of June 13 there was no "secret," strictly speaking. There was only the revelation—a symbolic one—of the Heart of Mary. This subject, far from being a matter for silence and reserve, was to be the very center of the entire Message of Fatima. The children, however, connected it with the vision of hell and the consecration of Russia to the Immaculate Heart. Hence the Heart of Mary was mentioned only very much later, when Lucia was ordered by her superiors to make it known.

The Chapel of the Sisters of St. Dorothy at Tuy
[Here Our Lady asked for the consecration of Russia
to her Immaculate Heart, June 13, 1929]

2

The Actual Secret

NOTHING PREVIOUS TO JULY 13, 1917 CAN BE CALLED, strictly speaking, the Secret of Fatima, notwithstanding the reticence of the children and their silence for so long a period. There had been so far no heavenly command concerning that silence, although there were many reasons, both natural and supernatural, why certain things were only much later made public. Lucia gives this explanation:

> After this apparition (of June 13), whenever they asked us if Our Lady had said anything else, we began to say that she had, but that it was a secret. But after July 13 we said that Our Lady told us that we were not to tell it to anybody, and then we were referring to the Secret imposed on us by Our Lady.

On July 13, 1917 Our Lady appeared for the third time. It was in this apparition that she communicated, among other things, what may truly be called the

Secret of Fatima. Let us examine carefully both the events and the message.

Our Lady began by teaching the children this beautiful prayer of reparation:

> Sacrifice yourselves for sinners, and say many times, especially whenever you make some sacrifice: O Jesus, it is for love of You, for the conversion of sinners, and in reparation for the sins committed against the Immaculate Heart of Mary.

As Our Lady spoke these last words, she opened her hands once more. The rays of light that streamed from her hands seemed to penetrate the earth, which opened most terrifyingly beneath the feet of the poor children. They beheld a vision of hell, of which Lucia has given us the following vivid description:

> ...we saw as it were a sea of fire. Plunged in this fire were demons and souls in human form, like transparent burning embers, all blackened or burnished bronze, floating about in the conflagration, now raised into the air by the flames that issued from within themselves together with great clouds of smoke, now falling back on every side like sparks in huge fires, without weight or equilibrium, amid shrieks and groans of pain and despair, which horrified us and made us tremble with fear. The demons could be distinguished by their terrifying and repellent likeness to frightful and unknown animals, black and transparent like burning coals.

When Lucia was ordered to write down part of the Secret, she called this vision of hell the first "thing" contained in the Secret. This was not written until August, 1941, but such was the impression the vision made on the sensitive little Jacinta that Lucia tells us:

"The vision of hell filled her with horror to such a degree, that every penance and mortification was as nothing in her eyes, if it could only prevent souls from going there."

At other times Lucia called the vision of hell the "first part" of the Secret. Of what do the other parts consist? Let us read attentively the following quotation, which must be given at full length, according to the original text which I have before me:

1. Terrified and as if to plead for succor, we looked up at Our Lady who said to us, so kindly and so sadly, "You have seen hell where the souls of poor sinners go. To save them, God wishes to establish in the world devotion to my Immaculate Heart.

2. "If what I say to you is done, many souls will be saved and there will be peace. The war is going to end; but if people do not cease offending God, a worse one will break out during the pontificate of Pius XI.

3. "When you see a night illuminated by an unknown light, know that this is the great sign given you by God that He is about to punish the world for its crimes, by means of war, famine, and persecution of the Church and of the Holy Father.

4. "To prevent this, I shall come to ask for the consecration of Russia to my Immaculate Heart, and the Communion of Reparation on the First Saturdays.

5. "If my requests are heeded, Russia will be converted, and there will be peace. If not, she will spread her errors throughout the world, causing wars and persecutions of the Church. The good will be martyred, the Holy Father will have much to suffer, various nations will be annihilated.

6. "In the end, my Immaculate Heart will triumph. The Holy Father will consecrate Russia to me, and she

will be converted, and a period of peace will be granted to the world.

7, "In Portugal, the dogma of the Faith will always be preserved; etc...."(*sic*).

8. "Do not tell this to anybody. Francisco, yes, you may tell him."

This extensive and important text of the revelations of Fatima consists of eight paragraphs. Their content must be pondered if we are to grasp perfectly what they actually say and what they leave to be understood.

In the first paragraph, the mystery of hell is connected with the establishment of devotion to the Immaculate Heart of Mary. Our Lady's intercession can obtain from God the salvation of souls who would otherwise be condemned. Note well that this idea already dominates the whole text. And we should not let ourselves be misled by the ideas which follow. Powerful as these may be, they are all subordinated to the salvation of souls by means of true devotion to the Immaculate Heart of Mary.

In the second paragraph there is a striking promise: the war of 1914-1918 will soon come to an end. It is a promise connected with the intercession of the Immaculate Heart. But if the world and the Church forget this, the text states that another war, worse still, will break out during the pontificate of Pius XI. When Lucia was questioned later about the apparent historical error, the Second World War of 1939 to 1945 having begun during the pontificate of Pius XII, she answered that the war had really begun earlier, with the annexation of Austria by Nazi Germany.

The third paragraph speaks of a sign to be given by God as a fore-warning of these events. Lucia saw the realization of this sign in the great aurora borealis at the beginning of the year 1938. She has never thought that this was a merely natural phenomenon. The war which began in September, 1939 could have been prevented—as we are told in the fourth paragraph—if two conditions had been fulfilled: Communion of Reparation on the five first Saturdays and the consecration of Russia to the Immaculate Heart of Mary. In the year 1917 Our Lady promised to return to ask for these two things. She fulfilled her promise to request the Communion of Reparation on December 10, 1925 in an apparition to Lucia, who was then a Dorothean postulant in Pontevedra, Spain. Today that convent has become a center of attraction for a deep Marian spirituality, and the faithful flock there from all over the world.

Our Lady made her second request, the consecration of Russia, in June, 1929, when Lucia was a professed Dorothean sister at Tuy, which is also in Spain. There has been much dispute as to whether the consecration of Russia to the Immaculate Heart of Mary has ever really been carried out in accordance with all the conditions required by Heaven. Sister Lucia is personally convinced that these conditions have not been fulfilled, although she humbly adds that she cannot know whether or not Heaven has been satisfied. From an historical point of view, it seems that the acts of consecration made by Pius XII and Paul VI to the Immaculate Heart of Mary do not fulfill the conditions Our Lady requested.

This is not the place for us to enter into further discussion of this important point, which we plan to deal with expressly in another book. If, however, we wish to ponder this aspect of Fatima from a theological point of view, we would say, first of all, that it is not in accordance with the theology of grace to think that by reciting a formula, perhaps in a mechanical way, we are going to obtain from God the conversion of Russia, as well as the immense benefits of peace which this would bring about. On the other hand, we cannot deprive of its "quasi-sacramental" effects a means that Heaven itself has proposed, above all when it has the support of a theology of intercession as secure and traditional as the intercession of Our Lady. This is undoubtedly why, in this case as in other cases in the history of charisms, the "intention" proposed by Heaven is the simultaneous application of the two extremes upon which God counts: on the one hand, our own conversion—that is, the conversion of Catholics who belong to the true Church—as a condition required for merit; and on the other hand, the consecration of Russia by the Pope and the bishops together with him, in the manner requested by Heaven.

The fifth paragraph describes in a very vivid and realistic way the punishment that will follow the "non-conversion" of Russia, if it has not been so consecrated.

The sixth paragraph, on the other hand, is typically

"eschatological," for the affirmations take on an absolute character, although always within the ambit of Christian hope. The triumph of the Immaculate Heart of Mary is absolutely certain, just as it is certain that "one day" the Holy Father will resolve to make the consecration of Russia as requested by Heaven. Will it all happen at the end of time, when all will be consummated? The text itself answers "No," since "a period of peace will be granted to the world."

Therefore, if the consecration of Russia, which will bring about its conversion and the great benefits of world peace, has not yet taken place, and the moment for the final triumph of the Immaculate Heart of Mary has not yet arrived, one conclusion is evident: we are living in an intermediate period, in which it is needful for us to purify ourselves, the world and the Church. Only in a spirit of penance, of compunction, of invocation of the powerful assistance of the Immaculate Heart of Mary will we be able to attain this definitive triumph for which we hope.

The seventh paragraph, presented by Lucia only in her fourth Memoir, contains what most certainly is the third part of the Fatima Secret. This remains unpublished, and we shall speak of it in Part Two of this book.

As for the eighth and last paragraph, this contains the command to keep silent about what has been revealed. Nevertheless, Our Lady adds kindly that it may be told to Francisco who, as we know, saw her but did not hear her words.

3

The First Two Parts

As we have said, neither in May nor in June of 1917 did the children receive any command from Our Lady to keep silent about the revelations being made to them. It was Lucia's prudent reserve, assisted by the Holy Spirit, that led them to understand that they should not speak about the promise of salvation and the practice of reparation to the Heart of Mary. Jacinta, unable to restrain herself, made known not only the first apparition, but also the promise of salvation. But in July, when they received the express order to keep silent about what had been revealed that day, Francisco and Jacinta clearly understood that they must not speak of reparation to the Heart of Mary because, as Lucia warned them, by doing so they might lead others to discover the Secret.

Jacinta, who was to die so young, could not, however, restrain herself completely. In her statements to Mother Godinho, which we regard as certainly authentic, she spoke much not only of hell, a subject that deeply distressed her, but also of the future of several nations. This is a most clear indication that what some critics called "new topics" were not really new after all.

The Secret which the children said they had received began to provoke curiosity and concern. The Administrator of Vila Nova de Ourem, Arturo de Oliveira Santos, thought that the Secret contained the whole mystery of the supposedly marvelous happenings. He therefore judged it necessary to use every possible means to extort it from the children. His first attempt was to order the children and their fathers to present themselves before him on August 11. Ti Marto, the father of Francisco and Jacinta, arrived without his children, excusing himself on the plea that they were too young. Two days later, on the thirteenth, the children were seized, but before carrying them off to Ourem, the Administrator drove them to the parish priest's house in Fatima, hoping to use the pastor to force the children to tell everything. The priest did indeed question Lucia about the Secret, but she refused to divulge it. Then, wishing to satisfy the priest, Lucia, in her ingenuous and childlike way, said to him, "Look, if you like, I'll be going there and I'll ask the Lady to give me permission to tell you the Secret, and if she says I may, then I'll tell you."

It goes without saying that during the three days the children were kept in Ourem, the Administrator and his colleagues were unable to extort the Secret from them, either by means of the most atrocious threats or by using flattery and alluring promises.

The Secret thus became the center of attraction for all the curious who came to question the children. After the death of Francisco and Jacinta, Lucia became its sole depositary. In June, 1921 she left the hallowed places of the apparitions and went to Vilar do Porto to begin the necessary task of her own formal academic and religious formation. While she was there her extreme reserve, which she continued with heroic faithfulness, allowed her to reveal nothing whatsoever about the Secret. Even during the interrogations in which she was most pressed, interrogations made by persons who had the approval of the Bishop of Leiria, Lucia always found a way of avoiding an answer to a question aimed at discovering the Secret. Here is a valuable text from Lucia herself:

> Almost all who questioned me were most impressed by the fact that, even while I was being interrogated, I lowered my eyes and concentrated my thoughts in such a way that I seemed to pay no attention to the question that was being put to me. At times, people even repeated their question, thinking that I had not heard it.
>
> I told Dr. Antero de Figuereido that I was recalling what had happened with regard to the subject on which he had questioned me. And indeed that was true. But the real motive behind my action was that I was seeking, in the depths of my conscience and with the help of the Holy Spirit, an answer which, without revealing the reality, would still be in accordance with the truth.

This painful situation lasted until the end of the year 1927. When, in December of 1925, Sister Lucia had an apparition of Our Lady concerning the great promise of the First Saturdays of the month, she did indeed disclose everything to her spiritual director and confessor, the saintly Father Lino Garcia. But she disclosed it in such a way that it would appear to have no connection with what happened at Fatima. She did this because she was awaiting a sign from heaven which would permit her to make known the great revelation of the Secret of 1917.

This sign was given in the following manner: Father Aparicio, S.J., who succeeded Father Garcia as Lucia's confessor and director in Tuy, realized, or at least suspected, that the revelation of the First Saturdays must be connected with what happened in Fatima. On a visit to Tuy in the first week of December, 1927, he ordered Lucia to give him a written explanation of the connection between the Heart of Mary and the events of Fatima. Lucia wrote:

On December 17, 1927, she went before the tabernacle to ask Jesus how she should comply with what had been asked of her, that is, to say if the origin of devotion to the Immaculate Heart of Mary was included in the Secret that the Most Holy Virgin had confided to her. Jesus made her hear very distinctly these words: "My daughter, write what they ask of you. Write also all that the most Holy Virgin revealed to you in the Apparition, in which she spoke of this devotion. As for the remainder of the Secret, continue to keep silence."

What was confided on this subject in 1917, is as follows: She (here Lucia is using the third person) asked for them to be taken to heaven, and the most Holy Virgin answered: "Yes, I will take Jacinta and Francisco soon. But you are to stay here some time longer. Jesus wishes to make use of you to make me known and loved. He wants to establish in the world devotion to my Immaculate Heart. I promise salvation to those who embrace it, and these souls will be loved by God, like flowers placed by me to adorn His throne." "Am I to stay here all alone?" she asked, sadly. "No, my daughter. I shall never forsake you. My Immaculate Heart will be your refuge and the way that will lead you to God."

This valuable text shows us that Lucia, at the end of December, 1927, was still hesitant and reserved about disclosing anything concerning the Heart of Mary because it was essentially connected with Fatima. Not, of course, on account of the connection in itself, but because she thought that to talk on such a subject at all meant walking on a slippery slope which might easily lead her into revealing the Secret of July, 1917, about which Heaven had as yet made no pronouncement. Hence her fervent question when she was before the tabernacle in Tuy on December 17, 1927, as quoted above. This is when Heaven gave permission, though this permission was limited and not complete. She was merely to state how the subject of the Heart of Mary had been made known in the second apparition in June, 1917. Nothing else was needed to enable her to carry out the order of Father Aparicio, and Lucia held to the permission given her by Heaven. We see, then, that the Secret of July, 1917 remained intact in Sister Lucia's soul.

The same thing happened when, at the end of 1935, she was ordered to write down her recollections of

Jacinta. How could she describe Jacinta's interior life if this little "Flower of Fatima" had lived so intensely a life of devotion to the Heart of Mary? Lucia saw the difficulty and prepared the Bishop of Leiria:

> Before beginning to tell Your Excellency what I remember of this new period of Jacinta's life, I must first admit that there were certain aspects of Our Lady's apparitions which we had agreed not to make known to anybody. Now, however, I may have to speak about them in order to explain whence Jacinta imbibed such great love for Jesus, for suffering and for sinners, for whose salvation she sacrificed herself so generously.

In fact this first Memoir, which so vividly describes how deeply Jacinta's life was marked with devotion to the Heart of Mary, makes no reference whatever to the rest of the Secret of July, 1917.

This occurs once again in the second Memoir. The Heart of Mary is spoken of, certainly, but the Secret of the apparition of July, 1917 is carefully passed over in silence. Thus we have already reached the end of 1937 without Lucia having disclosed anything at all about the first two parts of the famous Secret.

In December, 1940 Lucia, at the bidding of her directors, wrote to Pope Pius XII to ask him for the consecration of the world to the Heart of Mary. This is when Lucia wrote the paragraph which refers to Russia, its consecration, its conversion and the great benefits which would result from this: "In 1917, in Fatima, in that part of the revelations to which we give the name of Secret...."

Finally in the third Memoir, written in August,

1941, it is Lucia herself who explains to us all the details of both the occasion and the reason for writing down the first two parts of the Secret:

> In obedience to the order which Your Excellency gave me in your letter of July 26, 1941, that I should think over and note down anything else I could remember about Jacinta, I have given thought to the matter and decided that, as God was speaking to me through you, the moment has arrived to reply to two questions which have often been sent to me, but which I have put off answering until now....
> This will entail my speaking about the Secret, and thus answering the first question.
> What is the Secret?
> It seems to me that I can reveal it, since I already have permission from heaven to do so. God's representatives on earth have authorized me to do this several times and in various letters, one of which, I believe, is in your keeping. This letter is from Rev. Father Jose Bernardo Gonsalves, and in it he advises me to write to the Holy Father, suggesting among other things, that I should reveal the Secret.

The fourth Memoir, written in December, 1941, repeats the same text about the July Secret as in the third Memoir, except that it adds this phrase, which we have designated above as the seventh paragraph:

"In Portugal, the dogma of the Faith will always be preserved; etc...." (*sic*)

Within this section marked by dots was the third part of the Secret. To the origin, history and repercussions of this third part, we shall devote the second section of this book.

PART II

The Unpublished Part
of The Secret

*Jacinta, Lucia and Francisco after the apparition of
July 13, 1917, when they received the Secret from
Our Lady*

1

The Origin of the Secret

In Part One we have written about the different facets of the Secret of Fatima, in order to make the reader familiar with its inner unity, and to show that, just as many elements of the whole Fatima message were not disclosed for a time, so it was with the three parts of the Secret. The first two parts have already been made known, but the third part still remains hidden. It is of this third part that we shall now speak, in order to clarify its origin, its historical course, its repercussions and, as far as possible, its content and meaning.

As we have said, the first two parts of the Secret were definitively written in 1941. Halfway through 1943 Lucia fell ill. This led the Bishop of Leiria to order her to write down the remainder of the Secret.

Sister Lucia had always enjoyed good health, except that she occasionally suffered from bronchial trouble. At times this became acute, and she would be sent away for a rest, almost always to one of the peaceful low-lying estuaries of Pontevedra, La Toja or Rianjo.

In the summer of 1943, however, at the beginning of June, she fell sick with pleurisy. At first it seemed to be a mild attack, but almost immediately it became serious. She was running a high temperature. Lucia wrote to the Bishop, "Maybe all this is the beginning of the end, and I am happy. It is good that, as my earthly mission is drawing to its close, the good God is preparing my way to heaven."

By July, however, Lucia was recovering, but she soon became worse again as the result of an infection caused by a badly administered injection.

The Bishop of Leiria was concerned about Lucia's health, and even feared for her life. In July he wrote to ask her for notes which were to be used for a new edition of the little book, *Jacinta*, but when he heard of Lucia's relapse, he became anxious. Was Lucia about to leave this world and take her Secret with her? He decided to visit her and order her to write down the still hidden part of the Secret. Lucia had meanwhile contracted another infection, caused in the same way as the previous one, and was confined to bed. In spite of this, the Bishop went to Tuy towards the middle of September and spoke with her. They discussed writing down the remainder of the Secret.

Lucia's health began to improve gradually, but she suffered a suppuration in her leg, and an operation became necessary. She went to Pontevedra on September 21, 1943 and was hospitalized in Dr. Marescot's Clinic. This eminent surgeon operated successfully, and on the twenty-sixth Lucia left the clinic and went to the convent of her community located on the street called *Travesia Isabel II*, now known as the *Rua de la Hermana Lucia*. She stayed in the very same cell in which the Blessed Virgin had previously appeared to her. Early in October she returned to Tuy and gradually recovered her health, but this took some months longer, all through the year 1944.

It was in the midst of this painful ordeal of her illness that the third part of the Secret was actually written down, in circumstances that are worth recording.

Towards the middle of September, then, the Bishop of Leiria came to Tuy to speak with Lucia, who was confined to bed in the convent infirmary. As she herself has told us, the Bishop desired that she should write down the missing part of the Secret, "if I wished." This was not, of course, with the intention of publishing it immediately, but only to ensure that it be left in writing. The request, nevertheless, put Lucia in a quandary:

> It seems to me that to write it down is already in a way to disclose it, and I do not yet have Our Lord's permission for that. In any case, as I am used to seeing the will of God in the wishes of my superiors, I am thinking of obedience, and I don't know what to do. I prefer an express command which I can rely on before God, so

that I can say in all security, "They ordered me that, Lord." But those words, "if you wish," disturb me and leave me perplexed.

She decided, therefore, not to write unless she received an express command. As she said, even though it might remain sealed, it was still disclosed. Sister Lucia did not know how to decide between Our Lord's command not to write it down and the simple wish of the Bishop of Leiria, who left her freedom of choice. What is very interesting is the certainty which Lucia shows in her communications with Our Lord, so much so that these communications are her rule of life, provided other indications of the will of God do not intervene.

Once, when an assistant urged the Bishop to impose a command on Sister Lucia, he replied, "I do not interfere in matters of secrets." This time, however, there was a question of preserving the very precious third part of the Fatima Secret. The Bishop determined finally to give a command. In a letter written in mid-October, he gave the express order for which Lucia had asked. She showed herself perfectly ready to comply with the command, faithful and submissive as always. She was convinced that in obeying her superiors she was obeying God. She was often accustomed, however, to receive, as we have seen, clear confirmation from Heaven itself of such orders, and when on this occasion no such confirmation was forthcoming, Lucia suffered acutely. "Yet Heaven is now keeping silent. Is God wishing to test my obedience?"

All this happened during the month of November, 1943. At the beginning of December Lucia was in frequent contact with Don Antonio Garcia, who was still at that time the Apostolic Administrator of Tuy and already nominated as the future Archbishop of Valladolid. For some time past he had been giving Lucia spiritual direction at intervals, while entrusting her permanent direction to his Vicar General, the revered and holy priest, Don Jesus Varela. Speaking with Don Antonio Garcia, she confided to him her interior anguish:

> They have ordered me to write down the part of the Secret that Our Lady revealed in 1917, and which I still keep hidden, by command of the Lord. They tell me either to write it in the notebooks in which I've been told to keep my spiritual diary, or, if I wish, to write it on a sheet of paper, put it in an envelope, and then close it and seal it up.

Lucia expressed to Don Antonio Garcia the same fears she had spoken of to Dom Jose, the Bishop of Leiria. She told him that this order frightened her since, on the one hand, Our Lord had commanded her to say nothing to anyone and, on the other, His representative had told her to write it down. A real struggle was taking place within her. What should determine her decision? Begging Don Antonio to advise her, she added that she had several times wished to obey and had sat down at the table to write, only to find herself unable to do so.

No one could doubt that Sister Lucia's dispositions were good, even excellent. She wanted above all to obey. But faced with Heaven's perplexing silence, she felt that she had now become a stranger in Our Lord's eyes, and she suffered greatly on this account.

Don Antonio consoled Lucia and advised her to have patience, for the storm would surely pass. He also suggested that she write to Dom Jose explaining her difficulties in fulfilling his command. He urged her above all to remain calm, since she was in no way being disobedient to Our Lord.

Don Antonio's counsels were communicated to Lucia in early December. They are remarkable for the great prudence shown towards a soul in deep distress. Clearly there was nothing to prevent Lucia from writing down what had been commanded. Quite the contrary. Some writers have suggested that Don Antonio Garcia was greatly opposed to Lucia's writing the remainder of the Secret. There is nothing more unfounded. What Don Antonio advised Lucia was above all patience and much prayer, until this painful and perplexing situation should pass. He counseled her in particular to write to Dom Jose and express her difficulty in complying with his order. What Don Antonio wanted was to restore peace to Lucia's soul by assuring her that she was doing God's will perfectly. Could he have given better counsel?

Although Lucia was under the direction of the Bishop of Leiria, Don Antonio regarded himself, as long as she remained in Tuy under his jurisdiction, as "your prelate and pastor responsible for your salvation and sanctification." She was also at this time under the guidance of her superior, Mother Maria do Carmo Cunha Matos.

Is it possible that this mother superior, with questionable discretion, intervened to prevent Lucia from receiving the highly prudent correspondence of Don Antonio Garcia? Although this correspondence would certainly have delayed the moment for writing the Secret, it would have guaranteed an atmosphere of inner peace and calm. We suspect that this is what may have happened.

Don Antonio's letters to Lucia are dated within the first half of December, 1943 but Lucia did not receive them until the second half of January, 1944. By this time the Secret had already been written down, in the midst of very great spiritual difficulties. Did someone wish to prevent her from receiving these letters so that the writing of the Secret might no longer be delayed?

Lucia, without the aid of Don Antonio's letters, which had been intercepted, and with the feast of Christmas at hand, wrote to tell him that she had tried several times to write the Secret but was unable to do as she had been commanded. She added that this was certainly not the effect of natural causes. In another of her letters we learn that the Secret had still not been written by Christmas day. However, we also know that by the ninth of January, 1944 the third part of the Secret had been written. Therefore, even though our research up until now has not been able to determine the exact date, we know for certain that between December 25, 1943 and January 9, 1944 the famous final section of the Secret of Fatima, revealed on July 13, 1917, was at last written down by Lucia.

The only problem which still remained was that of finding a good opportunity to place the Secret, with all security, in the hands of the Bishop of Leiria. This took several months. Finally on June 17, 1944 the Bishop of Gurza, traveling with others who were unaware of the special mission entrusted to him by the Bishop of Leiria, arrived at the border of Spain and Portugal, at a place called Valencia do Minho. Lucia, who had come there from Tuy, gave him the precious document. That same afternoon the happy bearer of the long-awaited letter handed it over to Dom Jose when he and his companions arrived at the Bishop's country residence, *Quinta da Formigueira*, in Braga. The Secret had been written by Lucia on a sheet of paper, placed inside an envelope and sealed up. Later Dom Jose put it into another larger envelope, sealed that also and wrote upon it in his own hand:

> This envelope with its contents is to be given to His Eminence, Cardinal Dom Manuel, Patriarch of Lisbon, after my death.
>
> Leiria, December 8, 1945,
> +Jose, Bishop of Leiria

2

Incidents and Repercussions

THE THIRD PART OF THE SECRET OF FATIMA WAS NOW IN the hands of the Bishop of Leiria. Respecting absolutely the seal of the document, he deposited it in the safe of his chancery. It was never taken out except on very rare occasions, and then merely to be gazed at by a few privileged persons. Mr. Pazen, a reporter for *Life* magazine, was permitted to take a photograph of it which *Life* published.

These incidents, and especially their repercussions, have made Fatima "famous," thus constituting one of the more interesting chapters in the history of morbid curiosity on the part of the press and other news media, ready as they always are to jump at anything sensational and spectacular. It is necessary for us to clarify matters in order to free Fatima from the merely human elements which have so often made it appear ridiculous or have deformed it into a caricature which is utterly grotesque.

At the time the Bishop of Leiria received the sealed document, he was also given a letter from Lucia in which she made a few suggestions. One was that the document should be kept in his own possession until his death, when it was to be given to the Cardinal Patriarch of Lisbon. Following Lucia's suggestion, as though it were an order from Heaven, the Bishop wrote to the Cardinal. Later on, in a personal interview with the Patriarch, Dom Jose desired to entrust the letter to the Cardinal even before his death. The latter, however, refused to accept it. The document therefore remained in the chancery of Leiria until the moment when it was given to the Apostolic Nuncio in Lisbon, Msgr. Cento, to be transferred to Rome. Moreover Cardinal Ottaviani made a supposition which has every indication of being the truth when he said, "In regard to its being kept in Leiria, we can assume that Rome prudently did much the same as the Cardinal Patriarch when he was asked to accept it: that is they requested the Bishop of Leiria to keep it in his possession for the time being."

It also seems certain that, in a subsequent conversation, an agreement was made between the Bishop of Leiria and Sister Lucia that the document "would not be opened before 1960, or only after Lucia's death." A series of reliable statements compels us to consider this quotation as also true.

In the first place there is Sister Lucia's reply to Father Jongen. He put this question to her in February, 1946: "You have already made known two parts of the Secret. When will the time arrive for the third part?" "I communicated the third part in a letter to the Bishop of Leiria," she answered. "But it cannot be made known before 1960." The Bishop of Leiria, Dom Jose, also made similar statements. An example is his remark to Canon Barthas who comments as follows: "As early as 1946, when they were asked when the document would be opened, Lucia and the Bishop of Leiria both replied, with neither hesitation nor comment, 'in 1960.'"

Undoubtedly the Bishop of Leiria could have opened the letter immediately. But this holy and prudent man never wished to go beyond what Heaven had indicated through Lucia and he never broke the seals. Canon Galamba informs us, "I asked him many times why he would not open it. He always answered, 'It is not my duty to interfere in this matter. Heaven's secrets are not for me, nor do I need to burden myself with this responsibility.'"

"He could have read it," Cardinal Ottaviani tells us, "but he wanted to respect the Secret. He also acted out of reverence for the Holy Father." Dom Jose, where Fatima was concerned, placed all his confidence in Heaven, and he knew how to wait. When, in 1947, someone asked him if he knew the Secret, he replied, "No. I did not want to read it. Fatima is entirely God's work, and I did not wish to interfere in it."

The Cardinal of Lisbon, at that time Cardinal Cerejeira, an unquestionable authority, also made similar affirmations:

> From the two parts already revealed of the so-called Secret (the third part of which has not been made known, but it has been written and placed in a sealed

envelope and will be opened in 1960), we know enough to enable us to conclude that the salvation of the world, in this extraordinary moment of history, has been placed by God in the Immaculate Heart of Mary.

Other eminent Cardinals, undoubtedly well informed, spoke in like manner: Cardinal Tisserant, for example, and Cardinal Piazza.

The bishop who succeeded Dom Jose, his excellency Dom Joao Pereira Venancio, in declarations made at the beginning of the year 1959, said the same thing: "I think that the letter will not be opened before 1960. Sister Lucia had asked that it should not be opened before her death, or at least not before 1960. We are now in 1959 and Sister Lucia is in good health." Besides this, and without being influenced by any other so-called "clues," highly dubious in character, we find that Bishop Joao, who has had such intimate contacts with Popes John XXIII and Paul VI, took very seriously the message of penance that was made known in the Secret of Fatima. He proposed to all the bishops of the world that a day of penance and prayer should be held, from the night of the twelfth to the thirteenth of October, 1960.

Other bishops also spoke about the year 1960 as the time indicated for the opening of the famous letter. Thus, for example, when the Auxiliary Bishop of Lisbon asked Lucia when the Secret was to be opened, he always received the same answer: in 1960.

Canon Galamba is in complete accord with the authorities mentioned above. When the Bishop refused to open the letter, Lucia made him promise that it would definitely be opened and read to the world either at her death or in 1960, whichever would come first. "Lucia said only that it could be made known immediately, if the Bishop so commanded. But she did not say that it had to be opened immediately. The dates for making it known were determined in a dialogue between the Bishop and Lucia."

The one, however, who has spoken with the most clarity and the most authority on the subject is Cardinal Ottaviani who, as we shall see below, is one of the few persons who *has* read the Secret. Here are his words:

> The Message was not to be opened before 1960. In May of 1955, I asked Lucia the reason for that date. She answered, "Because then it will seem clearer." This made me think that the Message was prophetic in tone, for it is precisely in prophecy, as we so often read in Sacred Scripture, that there exists a veil of mystery..."Then," she said, "in 1960 it will seem clearer." The envelope which contained the Secret of Fatima was received sealed by the Bishop of Leiria, and however much Lucia said that he could read it, he did not wish to do so. He wanted to respect the Secret even out of reverence for the Holy Father. He (Dom Jose) sent it to the Apostolic Nuncio, then Msgr. Cento (now Cardinal Cento), who is present here. The latter transmitted it faithfully to the Sacred Congregation for the Doctrine of the Faith, which had asked for it, in order to prevent something of so delicate a nature, not destined to be given *in pasto* to the public, from falling, for any reason whatsoever, even accidentally, into alien hands.

We can deduce from this testimony of Cardinal

Ottaviani that it was Bishop Jose himself who received the order from the Apostolic Nuncio, Msgr. Cento. Dom Jose died December 4, 1957. When exactly was the Secret given to the Nuncio? By whom? And who took it to Rome? These are questions to which, without sufficient foundation, many diverse and even erroneous answers have been given. We ourselves can state with certainty that the document was still in the chancery of Leiria until the end of February, 1957, and that by the latter half of March it had already been handed over to the Nuncio in Lisbon. Why did the Sacred Congregation for the Doctrine of the Faith ask for the letter? Was it, as Cardinal Ottaviani affirms, because of some apprehension about its future fate or was there some other very different reason? We believe that there was indeed another reason.

Cardinal Ottaviani himself has told us that the Sacred Congregation was not interested in 1944 in having the document sent to Rome, preferring that the Bishop of Leiria should continue to keep it in his possession. Besides, at the beginning of 1957, there was no morbid atmosphere, still less a clamorous demand, that could have provoked such an intervention by the Sacred Congregation. It was not, therefore, an urgent desire to safeguard the famous letter that caused the Sacred Congregation to have it brought to Rome. What then was the real reason?

We know that at the beginning of 1957 the Sacred Congregation for the Doctrine of the Faith asked the chancery of Leiria to send photocopies of all Lucia's writings to Rome. This was done, and copies of the copies are still to be found in the archives of Leiria. What was to be done with the famous sealed document? Dom Jose, always respectful where he felt that Heaven's orders were concerned, did not wish to read it, or to photocopy it, for to do the latter would mean a disclosure not permitted before the death of Lucia or the year 1960. Most probably with an immense pain in his heart, he let the document go by way of Lisbon to Rome unopened. It had been confided to him by Lucia with the same affection with which she had entrusted to him all her writings.

When the letter arrived in Rome, it was placed in the archives of the Sacred Congregation for the Doctrine of the Faith, during the pontificate of Pope Pius XII. Pius XII did not die until October 9, 1958. Did he ever read the document? We ourselves feel that he did not, either because he did not think it was of sufficient importance—since it seems certain that in Rome in 1957 there was no apprehension about the Secret—or because he preferred to wait until 1960, and by then the Lord had already called him to eternal glory. What is absolutely false is a rumor that was already current in 1957, that Pope Pius XII did read the letter and that he wept because of the terrible things said in it. As Father Leiber, a close friend of the Pope, assured us, "That report is completely unfounded. There is not a word of truth in it."

In the case of Pope John XXIII, who succeeded Pius XII in 1958, we have more definite information. Pope John *did* read the Secret. Here is the statement of one who can speak with authority, Cardinal Ottaviani:

The Secret arrived in Rome and was taken to the Sacred Congregation for the Doctrine of the Faith. Still sealed, it was later, in 1960, taken to Pope John XXIII. The Pope broke the seal, and opened the envelope. Although it was in Portuguese, he told me afterwards that he understood the text in its entirety. Then he himself placed it in another envelope, sealed it, and sent it to be placed in one of those archives that are like a well where the paper sinks deeply into the dark, black depths, and where no one can distinguish anything at all. So really, it is difficult to say where the Secret of Fatima is now.

Cardinal Ottaviani was one of those permitted to read the letter. As he tells us himself:

I, who have had the grace and the gift to read the text of the Secret—though I, too, am bound by the secret—I can say that all that is rumored about it is sheer fantasy.

Since the first Spanish edition of this book was published in 1976, we have been able to gather additional information on the history of the Secret in Rome. These facts are now known:

The sealed envelope containing the letter was received by Msgr. Cento, the Apostolic Nuncio in Lisbon, from Msgr. Venancio in mid-March, 1957 and forwarded to Rome. It arrived there on April 16, 1957.

Pope Pius XII did *not* read the text.

Pope John XXIII received the document on August 17, 1959 at Castelgandolfo saying, "I reserve the right of reading it with my confessor." The latter was Msgr. Alfredo Cavagna.

The letter was read a few days after being delivered

to the Holy Father but in order to be absolutely sure about certain Portuguese expressions, the help of Msgr. Paulo Jose Tavares (later Bishop of Macau) was sought. The contents of the document were made known to the officials of the Sacred Congregation for the Doctrine of the Faith and of the Secretariat of State, and to a few other persons. It is certain that the Holy Father spoke about the matter with his close aides. However, he made no public statement. He simply said, "This makes no reference to my time," and left final action to his successors.

After reading the letter, Pope John did write a note which was transcribed by his personal secretary, Msgr. Capovilla, and included in the envelope containing the Secret. This was kept in the files in Pope John's quarters until his death on June 3, 1963.

We believe with all probability that Pope Paul VI also read the letter. We may likewise affirm that this had a decisive influence on his sudden decision to go to Fatima for the fiftieth anniversary of the apparitions, on May 13, 1967, and that the contents of the Secret are reflected in the homily delivered by him at the Pontifical Mass celebrated there.

3

A Great Disappointment

THE YEARS IMMEDIATELY PRECEDING 1960 WERE FILLED with an extraordinary and ever-increasing excitement as the public awaited the revelation of the Secret of Fatima. People were naturally anxious to know what was contained in the last part of the Secret since the other two parts were of such a nature as to suggest that the third part would contain something grave and serious. This attitude of curiosity and expectation was unfortunately exploited by some who should have been helping to educate popular piety in the direction of a more enlightened faith. As 1960 drew closer, unauthorized texts claiming to be the third part of the Secret began to be published in popular magazines and periodicals and to be circulated on mimeographed sheets.

As early as 1956 Radio Fatima had to deny rumors attributed to Lucia about prophecies of tragedy in connection with the Secret. The Portuguese periodical *A Voz* nourished popular curiosity by offering suppositions and suggestions about the Secret. One reporter went so far as to write:

> The first two parts have been public knowledge since 1942. The rest, by express command of Him to whose providence all things are subject, must remain hidden, for how long nobody knows. Until 1960? Perhaps. And what will be the contents of such a highly discussed document? Will it contain a complete revelation of the Message of Fatima? Shall we witness in 1960 some unforeseen and miraculous solution to the basic problems which divide the world into two blocs, east and west? Will it be the beginning of the period of peace promised to humanity, by means of devotion to the Immaculate Heart of Mary, in the form indicated by Our Lady? We do not know. Whatever it may be, the entire world, Catholic and non-Catholic, looks with anxiety towards the fateful year of 1960. The Holy See, on its part, also follows with the greatest prudence and attention, all that is happening as a result of the widespread diffusion of the Message of Fatima, for in all these happenings and manifestations the finger of God is very obvious. These phenomena are of such a nature and transcendence that they cannot be explained in human terms.

This atmosphere of excitement and almost morbid expectancy made things very difficult for the authorities at Fatima. When 1960 arrived they began to feel keenly that all these promises regarding the Secret were about to give place to bitter disillusionment.

A distinction was now made which formerly had not been taken into account. To open the letter was one thing but to make its contents public was another. This distinction seemed to be quite useless, however, for those who made it were contradicting what had been said earlier by persons in authority. When Dom Jose, the Bishop of Leiria, agreed with Lucia that the letter was to be opened in 1960, they obviously meant that its contents should be made public for the good of the Church and the world. Now the letter was no longer in the chancery of Leiria, so that the decision whether it should be opened and its contents disclosed to the general public did not depend on the authorities at Fatima.

Early in January, 1960 *A Voz* and the Rome correspondent of Madrid's *ABC* published a somewhat uncertain reference to the revelation of the third part of the Secret, stating that it would be made public during the year. The article said:

> Nothing is known at present. The Press, however, and especially the Italian Press, reflecting the curiosity and anxiety of millions of Catholics, asks when the famous document will be opened and made public. Many presume that this will coincide with the anniversary of Our Lady's first apparition, that is, May 13. Some assert that it is quite possible that the publication of the document may not be considered opportune, all the more so on account of the apocalyptic fantasies which are utterly unfounded, but which the authors claim to have learned from the lips of Sister Lucia, that the failure to reveal the Secret signifies the imminence of the end of time, or to speak more clearly, the end of the world at the hands of Russia.

Similar unfortunate rumors spread through France

as a result of an article by Francia Laffrey in the periodical *France-Demanche.*

With such rumors in circulation, it was not surprising that Fatima drew reporters from all over the world. Radio Fatima reported a typical visit:

> Yesterday, Mr. Giuseppe Gyreco, editor of the Milanese magazine *Grazia*, together with the photographer of the same review, Mr. Angelo Cozzi, were in Fatima in order to obtain information about the forthcoming revelation of the Secret. They interviewed the Rector of the Sanctuary, Msgr. Antonio Borges. They next went to Leiria, where they asked to be received by the Bishop, Dom Joao Pereira Venancio, being desirous of obtaining an interview with Sister Lucia in the Carmelo de S. Teresa, Coimbra.

It was inevitable that Fatima and the message of Fatima should suffer from such sensationalism. Early in February came the announcement from Rome which would stifle the excitement and as a result lead to a world-wide disillusionment with Fatima and all that it represented. The Portuguese news agency ANI reported the story as follows:

> According to Vatican sources (February 9, 1960), the Secret of Fatima will never be disclosed.
> It has just been stated, in very reliable circles of the Vatican, to the representatives of United Press International, that it is most likely that the letter will never be opened, in which Sister Lucia wrote down the words which Our Lady confided as a secret to the three little shepherds in the Cova da Iria.
> As indicated by Sister Lucia, the letter can only be opened during the year 1960.
> Faced with the pressure that has been placed on the

Vatican, some wanting the letter to be opened and made known to the world, others, on the supposition that it may contain alarming prophecies, desiring that its publication be withheld, the same Vatican circles declare that the Vatican has decided not to make public Sister Lucia's letter, and to continue keeping it rigorously sealed.

Does the Vatican already know the contents of the envelope? The decision of the Vatican authorities is based on various reasons: 1. Sister Lucia is still living. 2. The Vatican already knows the contents of the letter. 3. Although the Church recognizes the Fatima apparitions, she does not pledge herself to guarantee the veracity of the words which the three little shepherds claim to have heard from Our Lady.

In these circumstances, it is most probable that the Secret of Fatima will remain, forever, under absolute seal. (ANI)

Faced with the uproar caused by this announcement, it was necessary for the authorities to explain somehow the reason for not making the Secret public.

4

Why the Secret Was Not Made Public

TOWARD THE END OF FEBRUARY, 1960 THE CARDINAL OF Lisbon was interviewed on this subject by the newspaper *Diario de Noticias*. The reporter insisted, "Yet it was Lucia herself who had determined (and we believe that Our Lady of Fatima had wanted it that way) that the Secret should be made known in 1960." The Cardinal replied emphatically:

It is public knowledge that Lucia has had further supernatural revelations. Nothing can be said, however, about the time being opportune or inopportune for the publication of the Secret. I know nothing on this subject. Nor was I consulted about it. What I know about its publication in 1960 I have learned from the Press.

Cardinal Lercaro also, in his homily on May thirteenth, exhorted the faithful in the following manner:

We have come here, not moved by burning curiosity to know what other secrets our Blessed Mother's words hold for the world. We come, rather, repentant and deeply concerned that we have made so little of her admonitions. After so many years, we have still not followed her clear directives, nor have we responded to her loving petitions.

Not all the media were antagonistic. One newspaper reflected prudently:

> The final pronouncement on the Secret has been considered inappropriate, at least in the most generally accepted sense of the word, assuming that the last part of the message of Fatima might contain simply an invitation to prayer and penance in the spirit of the apparitions in the Cova da Iria.

This suggests, indeed, another plausible reason: if the Secret contained nothing new, then the reasons for not publishing it might be due solely to the agitated atmosphere which had arisen, which the Holy See would not wish to increase. An authoritative voice from the Shrine at Fatima gave similar advice: "Simple and generous souls must not allow themselves to be carried away by the sensational news which disturbs the world concerning the last part of the Secret of Fatima."

Later, in May, the Cardinal of Lisbon, with his usual eloquence, issued a pressing appeal to remain calm:

> Our Lady has already drawn, therefore, a picture of contemporary events, with persecutions in the Soviet Union and the destruction of certain nations. At the same time she has given us the remedy: the consecration

of the world to her Immaculate Heart. In these apocalyptic times, it is you yourselves who have the remedy in your own hands. Many are concerned about the revelation of the third part of the Secret of Fatima. They forget, however, that the essential message has already been given, and that is what we most need to know: that we are not to offend God and that we are to live in His grace.

The Bishop of Leiria, Dom Joao Venancio, also observed that people were beginning to think that the principal and most important part of the message was the part to be made known in 1960, whereas in fact the most important part was most certainly that which was already known.

It is easier to understand today the reasons why the Holy See did not reveal the Secret, and may never do so. To begin with, the circumstances which immediately preceded the year 1960 produced an abnormal atmosphere which made publication of the Secret inadvisable. To have acted otherwise would have been to contribute to the anxiety and state of panic caused by so many false texts, so many apocalyptic prophecies attributed to Lucia, and so much curiosity provoked by all sectors of the communications media.

Apart from this, there was the fear that the true text, once made known, would immediately be distorted by those who are ever eager to thrust before the public the most alarming news with the most sensational interpretations. Most importantly, Fatima and its total message would have been reduced to only this third part. People would have understood

Fatima as entirely an apocalyptic message, when it is far more than that. It was better, therefore, to wait for a time of greater calm and deeper understanding of the total message.

We might wonder, furthermore, whether it is reasonable to think that the Holy See would ever directly authorize the publication of a text on matters of such great delicacy. It has never done such a thing. The most notable example in history of such charismatic phenomena, that of the famous mystery of La Salette, remains in the Vatican Archives (if indeed it is still kept there) now almost a century and a half after it was written down, without its ever having been revealed. There is no serious reason for supposing that the Secret of Fatima is any more urgent than the Secret of La Salette.

Cardinal Ottaviani has told us that in 1944, when the Secret of Fatima was committed to writing, there was some suggestion that it should be taken to Rome, but that Vatican officials judged it more opportune to keep it in the episcopal chancery at Leiria. What will happen if, some day, Rome decides that the right moment has arrived for making the Secret known? Our own opinion is that the Holy See will not *of itself* make it public, but will find a reason, an "excuse" so to speak, for its being revealed elsewhere—by the Bishop of Leiria for example. To bring this about the document might, first of all, be returned for a time to the diocesan officials. We feel certain that the Holy See will never make public the letter which contains the third part of the Secret of Fatima. The reader will wonder, therefore, why the document was ever taken to Rome in the first place, and thus placed under Vatican jurisdiction. We can answer by saying that it would have been sufficient to send a photocopy of it, which was all that the Bishop of Leiria had originally been asked to do. But since the Bishop, Dom Jose, did not wish to open the letter, considering that to be contrary to an order from Heaven, he sent the precious document itself, still sealed, to the Sacred Congregation for the Doctrine of the Faith. We feel certain that today this document is a dead weight in the Vatican Archives.

The fact that Sister Lucia is still living does not seem to us a valid reason for not revealing the Secret. First of all Sister Lucia is still sufficiently shielded, exteriorly by the cloister and interiorly by an extraordinary fortitude, from all the assaults of public opinion, no matter what their source. Besides, this would not have been the first or the most important occasion on which she had to endure serious harassment on account of her writings. At the end of her longest Memoir, with an astonishing clarity of style, she writes:

I think, Your Excellency, that I have written everything that you have asked of me for now. Up to this, I did all I could to conceal the more intimate aspects of Our Lady's Apparitions in the Cova da Iria. Whenever I found myself obliged to speak about them, I was careful to touch on the subject very lightly, to avoid revealing what I wanted so much to keep hidden. But now that obedience has required this of me, here it is. I am left like a skeleton, stripped of everything, even of life itself, placed in the National Museum to remind visitors of the misery and nothingness of all passing things. Thus despoiled, I shall remain in the museum of the world, reminding all who pass, not of misery and nothingness, but of the greatness of the Divine Mercies. May the Good God and the Immaculate Heart of Mary deign to accept the humble sacrifices which they have seen fit to ask of me, in order to vivify in souls the spirit of faith, confidence and love.

If the Holy See did not consider it opportune to publish the contents of the third part of the Secret in 1960, who would venture to demand it? Who can presume to have greater knowledge of the circumstances in this matter than the Holy See? There have been people, however, who have demanded the publication of the document. They have done this, either in the name of serious scientific study of the history of Fatima (M. Laurentin for example, with great insistence), or because of the benefit souls would derive from reading it. The Most Reverend Balic, with an authority acknowledged by all in these matters, has pointed out:

A confirmation of such aberrations (concerning the credibility of private revelations) has been given to us by some priests and lay people who, while demanding the publication of the third part of the Message of Fatima, do not refrain from criticizing, in different ways, the ecclesiastical authorities. These persons seem to forget that it is the province of the Church, not only to preserve and interpret public revelation, concluded with the death of the Apostles, but to act in like manner with all that is connected with such revelation, as is indeed the case with private revelations. Only the ecclesiastical authority, invested with this power, has, consequently, the power and the right to judge whether it be opportune or not to make known a private and secret revelation.

Quite recently, in May of 1976, the Bishop of Marseilles said:

> Not a week passes without my desk being swamped with pamphlets recounting complacently interminable communications from the Blessed Virgin, or even Christ Himself, and reports of apocalyptic visions. Some people do not even know what to think any longer, and they go running off to wherever an apparition is announced, all the more persistent in their search precisely where the Church, after due investigation, has rejected such as unfounded. In San Damiano, this past March 25, more than four hundred cars could be counted....Just this very morning I received a tract campaigning to force the Pope to reveal the third Secret of Fatima, which "contains the solution to all problems."

Without excluding the other reasons that we have given for the non-publication of the document, we may now ask in a more pointed and critical way if it can be that the very contents of this famous third part are the principal reason for its not being published. We shall try to clarify this interesting problem, insofar as we are able, in the following pages.

5

The Content of the Secret

As we have pointed out in the Prologue, we would ask our readers, especially in what follows, not to expect from us any spectacular revelations. This does not mean, however, that what we shall say is simple conjecture offered without any guidance whatever. No, not at all. Here again our conclusions are well founded on solid reasons and historical inference which allow us to speak with the maximum probability.

That being the case, we ask our readers once again to pay particular attention to the spirit and intention with which we attempt to investigate the content of the third part of the Secret. We do not wish to make any concessions to unhealthy curiosity or to nourish a distorted interest in what is unusual or falsely supernatural. In no way do we desire to contribute to the sensationalism offered by the mass media. This book, and particularly this part of it, has a spirit and intention which are the very opposite of all this.

Our desire is to bring peace to souls, urging them to follow the path indicated by the third part of the Secret. We wish to calm and comfort them, but not with a false security, as though Fatima and its great promises could allow them to choose an indolent complacency that ignores Christian commitments. Quite the contrary. We want to give them serious reasons for not letting themselves be either carried away by false alarms or lulled to sleep by the conviction that "in the end, my Immaculate Heart will triumph." As we shall demonstrate in the third part of this work, the essence of the message of Fatima is that it inspires a hope that is a source of action, and a manner of life directed toward the coming of the Kingdom of God.

In order to speculate, with historical foundation, about the contents of the remaining part of the Secret of Fatima, it is necessary to take into account certain circumstances connected with the Secret as a whole, for these give us norms of interpretation for all hypotheses on the subject.

There is, in the first place, the marked brevity of the written Secret. Lucia tells us that she wrote it on one sheet of paper. Cardinal Ottaviani, who has read it, tells us the same thing. "She has written on one sheet of paper (*folha* in Portuguese) what Our Lady told her to tell the Holy Father." Some texts which have appeared, said to have been written by Sister Lucia, have left us convinced by their very length that they are not genuine. We shall speak later of this matter.

As for the general character of the Secret, as it was expressed by the good and simple people who questioned the children about it, we have here a few indications:

—To some ladies, of whom Maria da Capelinha speaks, who asked Lucia if the Secret was good or bad, she replied that for some it was good and for others bad, and that for her and her cousins it was good.

—The parish priest of Fatima, after many questions, only managed to find out that the Secret was not bad for the seers.

—Francisco, taken a little unawares by Dr. Formigao, admitted that the Secret was good for his own soul and for those of Lucia and Jacinta. He did not know if it was for the good of the parish priest. He said that if the people knew it they would feel sad.

—On the other hand Lucia, being more intelligent, replied that the people would remain just as they were before. When her mother urged her, in one last entreaty, to say whether it was good or bad, Lucia answered that it was good for whoever wished to believe.

Furthermore, as we have already shown, the Secret of Fatima has a "logical" content that is very clear and definite. As in all prophecy, it cannot be expressed except within its own literary *genre*, according to which certain future events can be fully understood only after they have occurred. Nevertheless, in the known parts of the Secret and in what is being fulfilled of the part as yet unknown, the mystery of Fatima is not a mystical text of an extravagant or nebulous nature. It has nothing at all to do with the Delphic oracles with their double and enigmatic meanings. Fatima is as simple as the rural environment in which the happenings took place. It also finds support in the real events which have disturbed our times.

From among the subjects which remained hidden at least for a time, and for that reason were referred to as secret, we may enumerate the following main themes which succeed one another in an interesting sequence:

1. The mysterious appearances of the Angel in 1915.

2. The wonderful apparitions of the Angel in 1916.

3. The early departure for heaven of Jacinta and Francisco.

4. The mission of messenger and apostle of the Heart of Mary, which Lucia received from Our Lady.

5. The fate of Maria das Neves and of Amelia.

6. The Heart of Mary in the interior life of the seers, together with their penances.

7. The Heart of Mary as a sign and a hope of salvation for humanity.

8. The vision of hell, revealed not for its own sake, but rather to bring out clearly the necessity of reparation and intercession through the Immaculate Heart of Mary.

9. Russia and her satellite states in connection with war and peace, punishment and promises.

10. The content of the third part of the Secret.

Of all these topics, only the last four, strictly speaking, actually formed the Secret of July, 1917. Moreover they were in fact the only ones that the children really considered as "mystery-secrets," inasmuch as they were the only ones that came under Our Lady's formal command.

As for the subject of the Heart of Mary, we have quite deliberately made a distinction between two aspects: one interior, the place of the Immaculate Heart of Mary in the inner life of the little seers; the other exterior, which we have called the sign and hope of salvation for humanity. The reason for this is that, in the July apparition, the Heart of Mary is to be seen in this important perspective. The following are the reasons for this division:

1. The first aspect, of an interior life inspired by the Heart of Mary, is proper to the first and second apparitions, though not exclusively. The children received the mysterious rays of light through a symbolic and interior vision of Our Lady, in which she showed them her Heart in symbolic form. This great light submerged them in God, whereas in July this same light gave them greater insight into the reality of hell and the Immaculate Heart of Mary as the sign and hope of salvation.

2. Their silence about the first aspect, as Lucia tells us, was never the subject of a command. But it came from such a strong and intimate spiritual force that it

was self-imposed. Keeping secret about the second part, however, proceeded from the very economy of the salvation of humanity, and it was Our Lady herself who commanded silence.

3. Finally Lucia began to make known the first aspect in 1925, though she was always careful not to become involved in the second, no matter how closely bound together they might be. She did not really write the second aspect with the intention of making it known until 1941.

It is necessary, therefore, to keep in mind these important distinctions if we wish to avoid committing serious errors when it comes to interpreting the message of Fatima as a whole.

Another important criterion for understanding the third part of the Secret is the unity of the three parts which constitute the communication of July, 1917. This criterion obliges us to discern clearly what is revealed and what is kept hidden, and also enables us to surmise, with reasonable probability, the nature of that which is held back.

The literary structure which Lucia adopts when she begins to write is quite clear: "Well, *the* Secret (italics ours) is made up of three distinct things, two of which I am now going to reveal." When, therefore, there is a question of hazarding a guess about the third "thing," it should not be disconnected from the other two as though it were a second thought that had been over-looked.

All authors have taken into consideration how Lucia, in the fourth Memoir, introduced the famous paragraph with the words: "In Portugal, the dogma of the Faith will always be preserved; etc...." They have deduced as certain that the third "thing" began there. These words introduce the revelation of the third part of the Secret. The phrase most clearly implies a critical state of faith, which other nations will suffer, that is to say, a crisis of faith; whereas Portugal will preserve its faith. That is why Lucia, in the enormous difficulty she experienced in writing this remaining third part, complained, saying that it was not necessary, for she had already said it so clearly.

Another very important point is the *intra-Church* nature of what was revealed as indicated by the very

Jacinta, Lucia and Francisco in August 1917
outside the Marto home

person to whom this third part was addressed. This, quite definitely, is what led the Bishop of Leiria to respect the Secret. It was the reverence he bore toward the Holy Father, to whom the Secret was addressed. This is what we believe to be most essential in the declaration made by Cardinal Ottaviani concerning the Secret. Let us read it attentively:

The world has lent an ear to Lucia's message, to that message which, over and above the parts which were private and personal, and the part which referred to the world as a whole, contained the third part of those things which Our Lady had confided to her, not indeed for Lucia herself, nor for the world, at least not directly, but rather for the Vicar of Jesus Christ...that which Our Lady revealed to her to be told to the Holy Father....The Bishop wished to respect the Secret, also out of reverence for the Holy Father....Yes, the Secret is important; it is important for the Holy Father for whom it was destined. It was addressed to him. And if the one to whom it was addressed has decided not to declare "now is the moment to make it known to the world," we should be content with the fact that in his wisdom he wished it to remain a secret.

6

What It Does Not Contain

WITH THE CRITERIA OF THE LAST CHAPTER TO GUIDE US, we are able to guess the content of the Secret. We shall begin by excluding that which it cannot contain.

In the first place, it does not foretell the end of the world or any great catastrophes or terrors to come, as certain texts referred to in the third part of this work would lead us to suppose. The reason for this is that the final triumph of the Immaculate Heart of Mary, which is something definite, will bring about an era of peace. It is true that it is said that "various nations will be annihilated," but the meaning of this may be purely political, and though this may prove to be "calamitous," it refers to a period which precedes the triumph of the Heart of Mary.

Replying to these very anxieties, Dom Joao Venancio, then Bishop of Leiria, made this observation:

The content (of the Secret) cannot contradict what is contained in the parts of the message already known since 1942. Wherefore, if the parts of the Secret already revealed cannot be in opposition to what we already know of the message, much less can they be in opposition to the Gospel. The Gospel tells us that God alone knows the time of the end of the world. The message of Fatima is not, therefore, a message of death, an incitement to panic and terror. It is an affirmation of life and hope.

Father Jongen asked Lucia the following question at the beginning of February, 1946: "Sister Lucia, do you think we are going through the period of Russian domination because Russia has not been specially consecrated?"

She replied, "I think that Our Lady's words are now being fulfilled: 'If not, she will spread her errors throughout the world.'"

Since, as we have said, Russia has not been *specially* consecrated, that is to say, in accordance with the conditions demanded by Heaven, we must conclude that we now find ourselves in that period in which all the punishments foreseen by Heaven are taking place. The triumph of the Immaculate Heart of Mary is yet to come. Finally a period of peace will be granted to the world. There is, therefore, no question here of the "end of the world," an event which has no part in the prophecies of Fatima.

The American author William Thomas Walsh asked Lucia in 1947, "Have you had any revelation about the end of the world?" Sister Lucia answered immediately, "I cannot reply to that question." Lucia's answer does not mean to indicate that she had had some revelation about the end of the world and did not wish to speak of it. She simply wants to put a discreet ending to questions which she is not permitted to answer. We must, therefore, exclude the possibility that the message has any specific relation to the end of the world. I say *specific* since in a general way the whole message concerns the last things and does indeed have to do, in that sense, with the end of the world.

We must also exclude from the content of the third part any reference to the previous apparitions or their fulfillment. We know, for example, that the apparitions of Pontevedra in 1925 and of Tuy in 1929 are complementary to what happened in the Cova da Iria in 1917. Events or complementary happenings of this kind must be excluded from the Secret. The context and literary structure of the text demand this.

We say this because some authors have speculated on the famous "seventh time" that Our Lady promised when she said in the first apparition:

"I have come to ask you to come here for six months in succession, on the thirteenth day, at this same hour. Later on, I will tell you who I am and what I want. Afterwards, I will return here yet a seventh time."

Today we know to what this seventh coming refers. Some thought it would be realized in a dramatic way, with Our Lady appearing in the Cova da Iria before an astonished multitude to manifest the truth of her words, "In the end, my Immaculate Heart will triumph." This notion is just one fantasy among many which have been attributed to Fatima and from which Fatima itself is so utterly removed. Lucia has explained that the promise refers to a personal apparition of Our Lady to her that has already taken place, in which Our Lady gave her the strength to go forward along the road that God pointed out to her through the Bishop of Leiria, Dom Jose. Fatima does not lend itself to cheap dramatizations in which the problems of the Church and of the world would be resolved by some sort of *deus ex machina*.

The same must be said of the reported revelations which were given on October 13 and which would have to be related to a *cosmic-theological* interpretation of the miracle of the sun. First of all these interpretations are wholly devoid of historical foundation. The text of the last apparition, which occurred on October 13, is well established, just like those of the previous apparitions, and does not admit of fantastic interpretations. Moreover Lucia has been a faithful and trustworthy interpreter of the text ever since that same year of 1917. We quote here what the parish priest said in his final interrogation:

> When she was also questioned about when Our Lady would appear again or when she expected to see her again, Lucia said that she was not expecting her any more, for she had promised to come six times, during six months—and these were already over—and she now hoped only to see her again in heaven.

When Jacinta was questioned on the same subject,

she answered with her usual brevity, "She said that today (October 13) was the last time."

We have already spoken of the complementary nature of the happenings at Pontevedra and Tuy. Here is the way Sister Lucia harmonizes these happenings with her statements that Our Lady's last apparition took place on October 13, 1917:

"I was referring to the apparitions on the thirteenth, in the form that they had taken in the preceding months. It was in this sense that I understood the question."

A few writers have taken as an authentic and therefore revealed text a letter from Sister Lucia to the then titular Bishop of Gurza. In this letter she tells him about some special communications which she has received from Our Lord regarding the fact that the consecration of Russia has not yet been made, and about Spain, the role of the Spanish bishops and the penance done in that country. None of this belongs to the text of the Secret, since this letter had already been made known and published.

We should remember in interpreting Lucia's writings that she never repeats herself in the same text, especially when she is dealing with related things. If therefore the first part of the Secret speaks of the vision of hell and the intercessory function of Our Lady to save sinners who would otherwise go there, and if the second part deals with the consecration of Russia to the Immaculate Heart of Mary, emphasizing particularly the disastrous effects failure to do so will bring to the world and the Church in their external, political and material aspects, then we can be certain that none of this will again be included in the third part. This criterion is important when we come to consider the general character of future happenings, made known to the Pope himself.

Finally, the message of Fatima is not concerned with wars or politics, except insofar as these form a sub-stratum to its own history of salvation. It is concerned, above all, with the intercession of the Immaculate Heart of Mary, shown to us as a "sign of salvation in these latter times." What is always asserted is that if this powerful intercession is not put forward in the Church as it should be, the Church will find herself exposed to most serious perils that will affect even her very dogmas. We therefore conclude as an important criterion of this question of interpretation, that what is proposed in the third part of the Secret must be in logical sequence to what went before.

Having put forward these criteria for excluding all that cannot constitute the remainder of the unpublished Secret, we now turn with a greater certainty to other, more positive criteria for discovering what it does in fact contain.

7

What It Does Contain

THE FIRST POSITIVE CRITERION, AND ONE THAT IS ABSO-
lutely certain, is the phrase which Lucia introduces
when she is writing the fourth Memoir in December,
1941. She had previously written this same text
several times, but *only here* does she use this introduction. Did she do this with the express intention of
letting the Secret be glimpsed and in this way
avoiding having to write it out? This is what the
phrase might permit us to suppose. She complains
about having to write the Secret because, "in a way, I
have already said it."

Let us now take a more thorough look at the
literary structure of the text as given earlier. We
divided it into eight sections. In the first is set forth
the very reason for the vision of hell: "To save them
(the souls who were going to hell), God wishes to
establish in the world devotion to my Immaculate

Heart." In the second paragraph we have the good or evil effects which will follow if this devotion is or is not established. Like all prophecies of the same type, this one is clearly of a "warning and conditional" nature. In the third section is given a visible sign for recognizing the times in which these things will be fulfilled. In fact the years 1938 and 1939 were years of "Machiavellian" scheming on the part of Germany and Russia, each trying to deceive the other. Hitler's coups and audacious moves finally alerted the Allies, while in the background Stalin was planning to betray both Germany and the West.

We need to mark well the material character of the evils that are to come: famine, war, persecutions of the Church and of the Holy Father. None of this, as we have said, will have to be repeated in the third part of the Secret.

In the fourth section there is express mention of the *radical* remedy: the consecration of Russia to "my Heart," and devotion to the Heart of Mary made more specific by the practice of the First Saturdays. This is also followed by a prophetic warning.

Logically it would seem that the sixth section should have come after the seventh, for it speaks of a later "definitive" period, whereas the seventh deals with a preceding "intermediate" period. The reason for this apparent contradiction is simple. When Lucia wrote the first version of the text, the seventh section was not given at all; therefore any allusion to the intermediate period was overlooked. But when she wrote the final version (in December, 1941) and introduced this disquieting section, she departed from the earlier versions already written, and the seventh part has therefore been placed where it is. Both the literary structure of the text, however, and the interpretations that Lucia has given us concerning it make its meaning very clear.

In the period preceding the great triumph of the Immaculate Heart of Mary, tremendous things are to happen. These form the content of the third part of the Secret. What are they?

If in Portugal the dogma of the Faith will always be preserved, it can be clearly deduced from this that in other parts of the Church these dogmas are going to become obscure or even lost altogether. It is quite possible that the message not only speaks of a "crisis of faith" in the Church during this period, but also, like the Secret of La Salette, that it makes concrete references to internal strife among Catholics and to the deficiencies of priests and religious. It is also possible that it may imply deficiencies even among the upper ranks of the hierarchy.

Lucia has several times spoken of the deficiencies of priests and religious. With regard to bishops, however, she gives proof of exquisite delicacy, saying for example:

> On account of all the sacrifice and effort of the bishops for the promotion of the cult and glory of the Immaculate Heart of Mary, and because they directly represent Our Lord, I have for all of them a great esteem, love and veneration.

When, therefore, Sister Lucia has some "communication" from Heaven for bishops, as for example for those in Spain, it cannot be regarded as a "charismatic excess."

Can the "intermediate" period of the text be identified as the one in which we are now living? We may affirm in general that this is so, for it is certain that the consecration of Russia has still not been made. On the other hand, the internal troubles in the post-conciliar Church bear witness to a lamentable state of affairs, clearly pointed out by Pope Paul. This has been characterized not only by conflicts and antagonisms within the Church, but also by a tremendous weakening in theological teaching and an excessively critical spirit that has undermined Scriptural exegesis.

No one can doubt that this is what has happened. But is it precisely to this condition that the words of the text allude, "In Portugal, the dogma of the faith will always be preserved?" There are assuredly good grounds for believing that they do. It is not, however, easy to say if the third part of the Secret refers to the era that we are living in today or to another epoch yet to come. To limit the "intermediate" period to the present time is extremely probable, but not certain. One conclusion does indeed seem to be beyond doubt: the content of the unpublished part of the Secret does not refer to new wars or political upheavals, but to happenings of a religious and intra-Church character, which of their very nature are still more grave.

It is thus understandable that Cardinal Ottaviani

should persist in saying that the Secret message was not addressed directly to the world, but to the Pope in person. Also it is easy to understand that prudence counseled the Pope not to add to the animosities within the Church between divergent tendencies and opinions. This is especially so since Fatima had come to be regarded as one of the *reactionary* elements of the post-conciliar Church; so much so, indeed, that Pope Paul's pilgrim-journey to Fatima was criticized by some as being a return to attitudes "superseded" by the Council. It is understandable also that the Secret and all its history should have been harshly criticized by the progressive element that has prevailed in certain sectors of the Church.

Moreover, how are we to understand Lucia's great difficulty in writing the final part of the Secret when she had already written other things that were extremely difficult to put down? Had it been merely a matter of prophesying new and severe punishments, Sister Lucia would not have experienced difficulties so great that a special intervention from Heaven was needed to overcome them. But if it were a matter of internal strife within the Church and of serious pastoral negligence on the part of high-ranking members of the hierarchy, we *can* understand how Lucia experienced a repugnance that was almost impossible to overcome by any natural means.

Still, the famous document must also contain elements of hope and promise provided that the Church, the hierarchy and the faithful turn to true prayer and penance and give themselves, in confidence and love, to the Immaculate Heart of Mary. It was Cardinal Ottaviani again who spoke with clarity on these points:

> The relationship of the message of Fatima with conditions in the Church in certain regions has become evident. In such areas, the attacks against religion are causing them to feel the weight of persecution. There, too, the message of hope and conversion exists, even before it becomes common knowledge, and this conversion can be hastened by the prayers of all who are devoted to Our Lady of Fatima....There are already signs which give us a glimpse of new situations which are beginning to appear. I may perhaps be optimistic, but it seems to me that the Holy Virgin is encouraging us to have confidence. These revealing signs are various indications of developments in certain countries, and of success in an ecumenism which is bringing peoples more closely together, even those who are not Catholic, but who glory, and justly so, in the name of Christian. Then there are signs of the success of all the Holy Father's initiatives in favor of peace....These are all signs which lead us to hope that, in this fiftieth anniversary of the events at Fatima, Our Lady wishes to give us a sign of her satisfaction with her children, to give new hope to the Christian world. We must say then: let us welcome Our Lady's desire, and let us hasten its fulfillment by prayer.

Cardinal Ottaviani alludes here to the fact that there also exist signs of hope in the Secret. He refers to two. First there is the conversion of Russia, of which he believes there are already certain indications. Next he refers to the ecumenical movement, as though there were also an allusion to this in the document. In regard to this second point, we should affirm that

Lucia has always thought that the *conversion* of Russia is not to be understood as being limited to the return of the Russian people to the Orthodox Christian religion, rejecting the Marxist atheism of the Soviets, but rather as a total and perfect conversion to the one, true Roman Catholic Church. In this sense, the ecumenical movement may find in the unpublished document a hopeful promise.

We have said at the end of chapter two of this part that we believed Pope Paul VI had read the Secret, and that this influenced his decision to be present at Fatima for the fiftieth anniversary of the apparitions on May 13, 1967. We have also given as our opinion that the Holy Father's sermon at the Pontifical Mass at Fatima reflected the contents of the Secret.

We would like to conclude this chapter by quoting that portion of Pope Paul's homily which seems to us to refer to the Secret. The Holy Father began by greeting the pilgrims, clergy and laity, who had come to Fatima from all over the world. He then continued:

> You all know our special intentions which have characterized this pilgrimage. Now we recall them, so that they give voice to our prayer and enlightenment to those who hear them. The first intention is for the Church; the Church, One, Holy, Catholic and Apostolic. We want to pray, as we have said, for its internal peace. The Ecumenical Council has revitalized the heart of the Church, has opened up new vistas in the field of doctrine, has called all her children to a greater awareness, to a more intimate collaboration, to a more fervent apostolate. We desire that these be preserved and extended. What terrible damage could be provoked

by arbitrary interpretations, not authorized by the teaching of the Church, disrupting its traditional and constitutional structure, replacing the theology of the true and great Fathers of the Church with new and peculiar ideologies; interpretations intent upon stripping the norms of faith of that which modern thought, often lacking rational judgment, does not understand and does not like. Such interpretations change the apostolic fervor of redeeming charity to the negative structures of a profane mentality and of worldly customs. What a delusion our efforts to arrive at universal unity would suffer, if we fail to offer to our Christian brethren, at this moment divided from us, and to the rest of humanity which lacks our Faith in its clear-cut authenticity and in its original beauty, the patrimony of truth and of charity, of which the Church is the guardian and the dispenser!

We want to ask of Mary a living Church, a true Church, a united Church, a holy Church. We want to pray together with you, in order that the aspirations and efforts of the Council may find fulfillment through the fruits of the Holy Spirit, the font of the true Christian life, Whom the Church worships tomorrow on the feast of Pentecost. These fruits are enumerated by the Apostle Paul: "love, faithfulness, joy, peace, patience, kindness, goodness, gentleness and self-control." We want to pray that the love of God now and forever reign in the world; that His laws guide the conscience and customs of modern man. Faith in God is the supreme light of humanity; and this light not only must never be extinguished in the hearts of men, but must renew itself through the stimulus which comes from science and progress. This thought, which strengthens and stimulates our prayer, brings us to reflect, at this moment, on those nations in which religious liberty is almost totally suppressed; and where the denial of God is promulgated as representative of the truth of these times and the liberation of the people, whereas this is not so. We pray for such nations; we pray for the faithful of these nations, that the intimate strength of God may sustain them and that true civil liberty be conceded to them once more.

The remainder of the Pope's address was an appeal to men everywhere to work for true peace in the world. While peace is of course a vital concern for the Church, it is also of concern to the rest of mankind, and therefore not the *intra-Church* matter to which we believe the Secret refers.

Bishop Correia da Silva and Sister Lucia as a sister of St. Dorothy

8

Fatima Disclosures Ended

THE ADMIRABLE DESIGN OF PROVIDENCE THAT HAS drawn the world's attention to Fatima and the fact that Lucia, after having written down the third part of the Secret, is still living and continues to write about Fatima, has led many people to think that the revelations of Fatima may not yet be ended.

We must therefore clarify a few points in order to gain a clearer understanding of the revelations of Fatima and of their meaning.

We should begin by distinguishing four ideas: the revelation itself; the writing down of what was revealed; its being made known to the faithful; and finally the interpretations made by Lucia, as seer and authoritative interpreter, as well as by others—theological writers and historians of Fatima.

The revelation itself closed with the last apparition of Our Lady in the Cova da Iria on October 13, 1917. As we have already said, the apparitions and visions of Pontevedra and Tuy are "complementary," destined solely to fulfill the promise of July, 1917. We can affirm therefore that the revelation of Fatima has come to an end.

The writing down of the Secret, on the other hand, followed a truly remarkable course and lasted from the first utterances of the children on the afternoon of May thirteenth until Lucia wrote the third unpublished part of the Secret sometime between December 26, 1943 and January 9, 1944. Lucia continually spoke of what this painful process of "being stripped of everything" meant for her as she committed to a blank sheet of paper the secrets which she had received from Heaven. For example, when she wrote the second Memoir, she said:

> I, the least of Your handmaids, O my God, now come in full submission to Your most holy will, to lift the veil from my secret, and reveal the story of Fatima just as it is. No longer will I savor the joy of sharing with You alone the secrets of Your love; but henceforth, others too will sing with me the greatness of Your mercy!

When, under obedience, she had to write the fourth Memoir, she spoke thus:

> Happy and content, I recalled the words I had heard long ago from the lips of that holy priest, the Vicar of Torres Novas: "The Secret of the King's daughter should remain hidden in the depths of her heart." Then, beginning to penetrate the meaning, I said, "My secret is for myself." But now, I can no longer say so. Immolated on the altar of obedience, I say rather, "My secret belongs to God. I have placed it in His hands; may He do with it as best pleases Him."

At the end of the Memoir she wrote:

To the best of my knowledge, I keep nothing back. I think I have only omitted some minor details referring to the petitions which I made. As these were merely material things, I did not attach such great importance to them....I think, Your Excellency, that I have written everything that you have asked of me for now.

When Lucia finally wrote the third part of the Secret, she said that she was "like a skeleton, stripped of everything."

In regard to the publication of all Lucia's revelations, there has been a prolonged and somewhat complicated history, which we cannot describe here. It will be discussed in detail in my larger critical work.

Finally, since the year 1944, Lucia has written and spoken a great deal about Fatima, which must be regarded as an effort to interpret the message. It is certain that Lucua, as seer, received the gift of prophecy, in the Pauline and Thomistic sense of the word, but it is by no means equally certain that she has also received the gift of the *interpretation of tongues.* Her testimony must therefore be examined with the greatest care. We may ask Lucia to recall Our Lady's words; but perhaps we should not ask her to interpret their meaning. As the Carmelite mother prioress so well expressed it:

The mission of Sister Lucia of the Immaculate Heart was to transmit Our Lady's message. She has done this magnificently. Do not ask her, however, to interpret what she has written or said. Ask this of the theologians, ask the hierarchy and the apostles of Fatima, whom the Holy Spirit raises up when and where He wills. *Ubi vult.*

The statue of Our Lady inside the Chapel of the Apparitions. This is the statue carried in Processions to and from the Basilica

PART III

The Meaning of
The Secret

Sister Lucia at Fatima, May 13, 1967

1

The Word Itself

THE SECRET OF FATIMA HAS ALWAYS EXERCISED A GREAT fascination. Even today, in spite of great disappointment that it was not published in 1960, it still continues to be a burning topic.

In this final part we would like to present some reflections on the deep meaning of the Secret. We do so because we believe that it belongs to the total mystery of the Fatima revelation. It must be treated with historical accuracy, as well as with reverence, as one of the spiritual realities through which God directs His Church.

What does the word *Secret* signify in the context of the events of Fatima and its message?

It is clear that the Mystery of Fatima is something whole and complete, comprising all the events and the full message. It is a great disservice to Fatima to take the "third part" out of the total content and call it "The Secret of Fatima," as though it alone contained the essential message. Fatima today, since it has received the approval of the Church, has its place within the wider context of the whole Christian mystery. Not, most certainly, that Fatima by itself constitutes this mystery, which is contained only in Sacred Scripture and Tradition, but because it is a living part of this mystery, helping to develop and unfold it. The mystery of Fatima is meant for the whole Church. It is one of the ways of living the total mystery that Christ deposited within His Church, a mystery which is expressed in sacramental forms and which is founded on those revealed dogmas which are nourishment for an intelligence illuminated by faith. Fatima is not an addition or an interpolation introduced into the deposit of Faith. It is not a secret or a mystery in this sense. Those who harbor the vain hope that the revelation of the Secret of Fatima will enlighten them on the course the future will take are completely mistaken. Fatima is, to be sure, a spiritual reality, but it is not meant to create either illusions or delusions.

Within the full mystery of the Church, the Secret of Fatima is somewhat like a fire of hot glowing embers which keeps its brightness hidden, as in a humble, simple hearth like the *lareira* which Lucia describes in her home at Aljustrel. There we may warm ourselves by the fire as it shoots out sparks intermittently during the long winter nights of the Faith, those nights which we must live in hope and love. Here we have, then, a first and basic meaning of the word *secret* as applied to the mystery of Fatima, which must never be forgotten as we discuss the problem of its content.

2

Some Explanations

THE SECRET OF FATIMA IS NO CHILDISH GAME. SOME writers, in trying to throw light on it, have given explanations which we consider unjustified. This is the case, for example, with the English author, Father C. C. Martindale, S.J., who has written of the events and message of Fatima with all care and respect, but whose conclusions do not seem to be warranted by the facts.

Father Martindale says, to put it briefly, that the Secret is simply a matter of concealment. Lived with great intensity, especially by Lucia, the message was "elaborated" until it was written down in the form in which we now have it. Human curiosity, he says, has fastened on the Secret and wondered what is in the unopened document. Now the first two parts of the Secret contain nothing new. Hell is no new doctrine; nor that Our Lady is immaculate. It is not novel or startling *information* that Our Lady proposed to impart to us, but rather a challenge to look more deeply into what we already know. It need not surprise us, continues Father Martindale, that the children were told to say nothing about what Our Lady said to them; Lucia quite frankly said that she would not have had words in which to express herself properly, and that she could give only the "sense" of Our Lady's message. This, he concludes, encourages one to think that the secrecy of the message may have concerned the *intensity* with which the children were made to understand certain truths, rather than anything which could be crystallized or put into words.

In this interpretation there is an element of truth which must be preserved. The reason for the children's silence *is* to be explained more by the intensity with which they lived the Secret than by definite instructions from Our Lady. But it is clear that this cannot constitute the truly confidential sense of what has been revealed. In the same way that Christian dogma has a conceptual content which cannot be removed from it under pain of reducing it to vague sentiment, so the nature of the Secret cannot be reduced to a mere *living* of its content, however intense this living may be. The Secret of Fatima has a very concrete meaning. To suppose that this is merely a later work of subjective "elaboration" on Lucia's part is to refuse to understand the facts *historically*, merely inventing working hypotheses that do not have any foundation in the documents.

Another author, Father Veloso, whose difficulties are similar to those of Father Martindale, offers another solution. If the existence of hell is already a well-known dogma, how can it be the object of a Secret? He answers that the word *secret* does not express only a truth which is hidden. It also signifies a hidden meaning, an explanation, a motive, a key. Father Veloso states, "The Secret of the conversion of sinners was the children's suffering, their prayer and their consecration to the Immaculate Heart of Mary." Thus, he says, it is in this sense that the Secret concerning the vision of hell must be interpreted; that is, the hidden reason, the key to the message of Fatima is precisely the existence of hell, which is the Secret of all that has happened and is still happening in Fatima.

This explanation reduces the content of the Secret of Fatima to that of the motivating force which its truths possess. It detracts from the true meaning of

The first Chapel at Fatima, begun in 1918

the Secret by making hell the singular motivating force of Fatima's influence. This is obviously false; the reason for the vision of hell is not to be found in itself but rather in what immediately follows: "You have seen hell where the souls of poor sinners go. To save them, God wishes to establish in the world devotion to my Immaculate Heart." The true reason for the vision is to establish devotion to the Immaculate Heart of Mary. The message of Fatima is based on a constructive and positive theology which gives rise to an open and progressive spirituality, not to one that is paralyzing and based on fear.

In place of these opinions given above, we would like to propose the following definition of the Secret of Fatima:

The Secret of Fatima, in a broad but true sense, is the entire mystery of Fatima presented by its events and written texts taken as a whole, and seen in the total unity with which they were given to the Church.

In a more specific sense it is the special content, held back and kept hidden by a providential disposition of Heaven, which the little seers did not wish to make known except very gradually.

3

The Meaning of the Secret

THE SECRET OF FATIMA IS NOT A MERE MYSTICAL EXPERI-
ence, without historical or conceptual content. It has
a meaning. We cannot imagine it as a game of chance
or a deception devised by men. Without doubt it is
part of that special providence with which God has
directed everything concerning Fatima.

We begin by affirming its historical foundation.
Fatima cannot simply be relegated to legend, for it is a
contemporary fact. Nor can it be classified with
mythical accounts, for however much we may purify
the concept of *myth*, it is difficult to apply it to a
history which can be described in detail.
Furthermore, the Secret of Fatima comes from the
children themselves, and not from an over-excited
popular imagination which would, of necessity, have
exaggerated the facts and have made myths out of
them.

The Fatima children, when they speak of the Secret, are not playing a game, but rather presenting us with something very serious which they zealously guard against all interference on the part of parents and relatives, neighbors and companions, priests and bishops, and against the flattery, threats and promises of the civil authorities.

The Secret of Fatima is not a secret in the sense of being a new doctrine, something original which has come to revolutionize dogma, morals or Christian spirituality. All the dogmatic and spiritual riches of the message of Fatima belong to the purest tradition of the Church. In this sense, Fatima is completely *Catholic.*

The entire message, however, is the "Secret of Fatima," in the sense that Fatima has given it to the Church in a new spiritual experience. In Fatima the Gospel has become living and tangible.

4

Decadent Apocalyptic Literature

THE SPIRITUAL PHENOMENA WE CALL "PRIVATE REVELA-tions" do not have as their specific purpose the devel-opment of Christian dogma, but rather the preserva-tion of the Faith and Christian morality. They not only continue the Church's prophetic and historical tradition, but are also in accord with the very nature of the pilgrim Church.

Nevertheless there is a fact which must be empha-sized. Side by side with these genuine private revelations, there are often found other details which imitate them but are in reality a deformation and a caricature. In this way the original message is com-promised, and shadows are sometimes cast on the very authenticity of the events themselves.

This has happened to almost all private revelations, even those that are authenticated both theologically and historically. We know, for example, how the "secret" of Melanie and Maximin of La Salette gave rise to the most incredible speculations. We are aware also of the unhealthy curiosity that developed in regard to the personal secrets of Bernadette of Lourdes.

The events of Fatima also, whenever they are not seen in their true light, become the prey all too easily of bizarre notions of the "marvellous" and of a decadent kind of "doomsday" commentary. The fact that the message was given in several apparitions instead of one, the insistence on the Secret and its three parts, the relationship between Fatima and Russia, the connection with the two world wars, the indiscretions and publicity attached to the scheduled publication of the third part of the Secret in 1960, the survival of Lucia to the present time and perhaps some of her own declarations—all these constitute more than sufficient motive for the creation of an "apocalyptic" atmosphere, one highly unsuited to growth in the Faith or to any true understanding of Fatima and its message.

Is Fatima itself at fault? Was it possible to restrain popular imagination with its passion for excitement and sensationalism? Even more, is Fatima responsible for the development during recent years of a climate of opinion hostile to Fatima itself, as a result of the reticence of some in holding back publication of the documents, and the imprudence of others in promising their publication when they had no authority to do so?

We cannot blame the *true* Fatima and its message

for such excesses. We can affirm, however, that almost from the beginning the events of Fatima have been accompanied by a succession of texts and messages, all completely spurious. It would be impossible to mention them all. We shall confine ourselves, therefore, only to the most important of them, and especially to the most recent.

Popular sensationalism was fully exploited in the very first newspaper account that we have on Fatima. It is from the Portuguese *O Seculo* of July 23, 1917:

> Everyone's curiosity was running high, and for a few moments they all remained silent, open-mouthed and intent, as though seeking to hear a voice come forth from the bowels of the earth. Then was heard a noise like the crash of thunder, and at once, from near the holm-oak which was all decorated with flowers—from paradise, I think—the two little girls burst forth into loud weeping, making convulsive gesticulations, and then fell into ecstasy.

Another secular newspaper, *O Mundo* of August 19, 1917, elaborated on the terrifying aspects of punishment:

> This is just one more example, a symbol of the purity that came to save the world through goodness, yet at the same time threatened to denounce those who did not wish to believe in her virtues....Fatima, too, preaches hatred.

Sensationalism of this kind flourishes, of course, in cheap literature. The journalist Avelino de Almeida prepared readers of *O Seculo* for what was to happen on October 13, 1917 as follows:

The phenomenology of the apparitions is the same as ever, the latest and most ornate flowering of that luxuriant genealogical tree of Marian cult, which spread forth its branches through the Pyrenees and the Alps, at Ousse, Medoux, Garaison, La Salette. Just as in 1500, in 1648, and in 1858, it is once more to poor, humble and ignorant children that the vision makes herself known, recommending prayer and appealing to the multitudes to gather there and offer her homage....

Others, however, in the divinely solemn moment, see the stars twinkling in the blue sky, even though the sun is at its zenith. They hear underground rumblings which announce the presence of the Lady; they say the temperature has dropped and some compare what they experience to their impressions at the moment of a solar eclipse....The faces of some are covered with the pallor of death.

Later on there were speculations about the early deaths of two of the seers, and about Lucia's inexplicable disappearance, when she had gone to a boarding school at Vilar.

The great bulk of such sensational literature, of course, was connected with the third part of the Secret, which remained unpublished and which most authorities declared would be opened in 1960.

5

False Texts of the Secret

IT WAS IN AN ATMOSPHERE SATURATED WITH SUCH UN-
healthy curiosity and speculation that many texts
began to appear between 1954 and 1960, claiming to
be the true and genuine Secret of Fatima. There were
a great many of these but we shall mention only the
three principal ones because these still cause a good
deal of confusion and fill the minds of the faithful
with anxious foreboding which is harmful to the true
Faith and to Fatima's message of light and hope.
These three texts have been published under the
authority of Father Lombardi, Father Fuentes and a
German writer, Ludwig Emrich. If we make personal
mention of these names, it is because they have
received such enormous publicity that it would be
absurd to omit them.

Besides, the critical intention which leads us to
form a judgment on these three authors is intended to

be constructive. Our aim is to point out in these texts precisely what is positive and what is negative, and to suggest that some of the negative elements were perhaps introduced at a later date by very inaccurate reproductions of the original documents.

Taking these writings in chronological order, the first is that of Father Lombardi, who is well known throughout the world as the founder of the "Better World Movement." On February 7, 1954 Father Lombardi, after much insistence, but at an inopportune time for Sister Lucia, managed to speak with her in the parlor of the Carmelite convent in Coimbra. He wrote later of the impression she made on him:

> Her face was simple, her voice clear and without the slightest trace of the artificiality which can be so easily assumed in certain situations. She was not well; in fact, she was running a temperature. I questioned her:
>
> "Tell me if the Better World Movement (which was already known to her) is the Church's response to the words Our Lady spoke to you."
>
> "Father," she replied, "there is certainly need of this great renewal. Without it, and considering the present state of humanity, only a limited part of the human race will be saved."
>
> "Do you really believe that many people go to hell? I myself hope that God will save the greater number, and I even wrote it in a book entitled *The Salvation of Those Who Have No Faith.*"
>
> "Father, many are condemned."
>
> "It is certain that the world is an abyss of vice....Still, there is always hope of salvation."
>
> "No, Father, many, many are lost."

Father Lombardi reminds his readers that Lucia has

had a vision of hell. He returned to Italy with this grave warning in his heart, and with a firm resolve to continue with still greater energy in spreading the Better World Movement.

The reader will have observed that there is not a single mention of the Secret of Fatima in Lucia's words, and for this reason our first conclusion must be that all the apprehensions to which Father Lombardi's account of his conversation with Lucia gave rise cannot be based on any frightening interpretation of the Secret. Besides, are these apprehensions in harmony with what Lucia has written on other occasions about hell?

We already know the text of the vision of hell. It does not say one single word as to whether the damned are few or many. Lucia tells us of the impression this vision made upon little Jacinta. When she wishes to explain Jacinta's spirit of mortification for sinners—for whose salvation she suffered so intensely—Lucia gives us two reasons: "First, because God willed to bestow on her a special grace, through the Immaculate Heart of Mary, and second, because she had looked upon hell, and had seen the ruin of souls who fall into it." Jacinta was profoundly impressed and exclaimed, "We must pray very much to save souls from hell! So many go there! So many!" In the same Memoir we see how Jacinta had visions of the war and of the many dead. Lucia asked her, "Jacinta, what are you thinking about?" "About the war that is coming. So many people are going to die, and almost all of them are going to hell!"

In Lucia's conversation with William Thomas Walsh there is this question: "Our Lady showed you many souls going to hell. Did you get the impression from her that more souls are damned than saved?" This amused Lucia a little. "I saw those that were going down. I didn't see those who were going up!"

These are the texts that we have before us. It is true that little Jacinta, who was so deeply impressed, used that awe-inspiring expression which has horrified so many people. But do we have to take it literally? As far as Lucia is concerned, there is nothing to justify the reactions of alarm aroused by Father Lombardi's account. In any event it is certain that none of this pertains to the Secret of Fatima.

Father Fuentes' text is more complicated, and it was immediately circulated around the world in thousands and thousands of different versions, all provoking countless states of alarm. There are three questions we must ask about it. Was the fault entirely his? What was the original text? Can it be attributed to Lucia?

Father Fuentes, a Mexican priest who had been appointed vice-postulator of the Causes for the beatification of Francisco and Jacinta, had a conversation with Lucia on December 26, 1957. On returning to Mexico, he gave a conference on May 22, 1958, in which he gave an account of his interview. We possess two authentic texts of this conference, one in Spanish and the other in English, the latter an abbreviated translation, but identical in its essentials with the Spanish text.

Father Fuentes begins by speaking of a message received from the lips of Lucia herself:

I would like to tell you only of the last conversation I had with her, which took place on the twenty-sixth of December last.

When I visited Sister Lucia in her convent, I found her very concerned, pale, far from well. The first thing she said to me was, "Father, the Blessed Virgin is very sad because no one heeds her message, neither the good nor the bad. The good continue in their life of virtue, but without paying any attention to the message of Fatima. Sinners keep following the road of evil, because they fail to see the terrible chastisement that is about to befall them. Believe me, Father, God is going to punish the world, and very soon. The chastisement of heaven is imminent. In less than two years 1960 will be here, and what will happen then? If we do not pray and do penance, it will be very grievous for all of us. Our Lady has said repeatedly, 'Many nations will disappear from the face of the earth, and Russia will be the instrument of heaven's chastisement for the entire world, unless we obtain the conversion of that poor nation.'"

Sister Lucia continued, "Father, the devil is carrying on a decisive battle with the Virgin Mary. He sees that his time is getting short, and he is making every effort to gain as many souls as possible. He wants to get hold of consecrated souls."

Sister Lucia said to tell everyone that what led her cousins, Jacinta and Francisco, to make so many sacrifices was that Our Lady looked so sad, and never smiled during the apparitions. The vision of hell was for them a further source of sanctification. Her sadness because of the offenses against God and the punishment in store for sinners so impressed the children that they ran ever more generously along the road of prayer and sacrifice.

Sister Lucia also said to me, "Father, let us not expect the Holy Father to make a general summons to do penance, nor let us expect a general summons from our bishops and our religious superiors. Let each one begin with his own spiritual reform. It is a personal responsibility toward God. With prayer and penance, we will not only save ourselves, but likewise all those whom God has placed in our path.

"Our Lady did not tell me," Lucia said, "that we are living in the last epoch of the world, but she did give me to understand that, firstly, we are going through a decisive battle, at the end of which we will be either of God or of the evil one: there will be no middle way; secondly, that the last means God will give to the world for its salvation are the Holy Rosary and the devotion to the Immaculate Heart of Mary; and thirdly, when God, in His providence, is about to chastise the world, He first uses every means to save us, and when He sees we have not made use of them, then He gives us the last anchor of salvation, His Mother.

"Father, with the new efficacy Our Lady has given to the Rosary, there is no problem in the life of any one of us which cannot be solved by frequently praying the Rosary. With the Rosary we will be saved, we will be sanctified, we will console Our Lord, and we will obtain the salvation of many souls. In devotion to the Immaculate Heart of Mary, we approach the seat of clemency, goodness and pardon, and find there a secure way to heaven."

We do not transcribe here the second part of Father Fuentes' report since it refers to the personal sufferings Pope Pius XII faced because of the situation of the world and the Church.

These are excerpts from the genuine text of what Father Fuentes has inappropriately called *A Message from Lucia*. It was published, in both the original Spanish and the English translation, with every guarantee of authenticity and with due episcopal approval, including that of the Bishop of Leiria. Later on, however, this text was completely distorted even though, in itself, the original was indeed worthy of reflection by Christian people. When the text was printed in other periodicals of popular piety, it was drastically changed, to the point of being utterly deformed. This gave rise to a variety of spurious versions which belonged neither to Lucia nor even to Father Fuentes. In these widely publicized, but inaccurate texts, all the cataclysms of the latter times were predicted in the most grotesque manner.

When these world-shaking texts reached Portugal, the bishop's office in Coimbra intervened with an official statement condemning them strongly:

> For the peace of mind of those who have read the documentation published in *A Voz* and have taken alarm at the thought of fearful cataclysms which, according to such documentation, are to come upon the world in 1960, and still more, in order to put an end to the biased campaign of "prophecies," whose authors, perhaps without realizing it, are provoking a storm of ridicule, not only where they themselves are concerned, but also with regard to things reported as having been said by Sister Lucia, the Diocese of Coimbra has decided to publish these words of Sister Lucia, given in answer to questions put by one who has the right to do so:
>
> "Father Fuentes spoke to me in his capacity as Postulator for the Causes of Beatification of the Servants of God, Jacinta and Francisco Marto. We spoke solely of things connected with this subject; therefore, whatever else he refers to is neither exact nor true. I am sorry about it, for I do not understand what good can be done

for souls when it is not based on God, who is the Truth.
I know nothing, and could therefore say nothing, about
such punishments, which are falsely attributed to me."

Who was right in this lamentable affair? Father
Fuentes, the Coimbra diocesan spokesman or Lucia?
We would like to offer an explanation, giving our
own modest opinion:

1. What Father Fuentes says in the *genuine* text of
his conference to the Mexican religious community in
December, 1957 corresponds no doubt in its *essentials*
to what he heard during his visit to Sister Lucia, for
although the report is mingled with the preacher's
own oratorical embellishments, and although it is
adjusted to conform to a literary pattern, these texts
say nothing that Sister Lucia had not said in her
numerous published writings. Perhaps the principal
defect lay in the presentation of these texts *as coming
from Lucia's own mouth*, and formally and expressly
given as "a message from her" to the world. Sister
Lucia did not have this intention.

2. The genuine text, *the only one that can be justly
attributed to Father Fuentes*, does not, in my opinion,
contain anything that could give rise to the condem-
natory notice issued from Coimbra. On the contrary,
it contains a teaching most suited to edify the piety of
Christians.

3. The diocese of Coimbra, and through it Sister
Lucia, have made no distinction between the genuine
text which can alone be justly attributed to Father
Fuentes, and the vast "documentation" to which we
have already referred. An error of judgment was thus

committed, for everything was included in one single all-embracing condemnation.

The proliferation of spurious texts about the Secret of Fatima did not end here, however. On October 15, 1963 a German weekly published a long and sensational article which claimed to be a reproduction of the text of the Secret.

The circumstances reported were highly spectacular. It was stated that the text had been communicated by Pope Paul VI to the leading heads of state—Macmillan, Kennedy and Krushchev—and had made such an impression on the three statesmen that it had decisively influenced their agreement of August 6, 1963 on the cessation of atomic tests in the air, on land and under the ocean. We reproduce here the most significant part of the text, translated from the German original of *Neues Europa*, No. 20, October 15, 1963:

Today, however, we are able to give to our international circle of readers of *Neues Europa* the content of the third message of Fatima in fragmentary form, that is, in the form made accessible by inside information in diplomatic circles of Washington, London and Moscow....Although in the document we are not dealing with the original text of the message of Fatima, as it was revealed by the Mother of God on October 13, 1917, to the seer Lucia, the document does contain, notwithstanding, the essential points of the original. It reads as follows:

"It was the thirteenth of October, 1917. On that day, the Holy Virgin appeared for the last time to the little visionaries, Jacinta, Francisco and Lucia, at the end of a series of six apparitions in all. After the manifestation of the miracle of the sun at Fatima, the Mother of God revealed a special secret message to Lucia, in which she particularly stated:

'Don't worry, dear child. I am the Mother of God speaking to you and begging you to proclaim in my name the following message to the entire world. In doing this, you will meet great hostility. But be steadfast in the Faith and you will overcome this hostility. Listen, and note well what I say to you: Men must become better. They must implore the remission of the sins which they have committed, and will continue to commit. You ask me for a miraculous sign so that all may understand the words in which, through you, I address mankind. This miracle which you have just seen was the great miracle of the sun! Everyone has seen it—believers and unbelievers, country and city dwellers, scholars and journalists, laymen and priests. And now, announce this in my name:

'A great punishment shall come to all mankind, not today as yet, nor even tomorrow, but in the second half of the twentieth century. What I have already made known at La Salette through the children Melanie and Maximin, I repeat today before you. Mankind has not developed as God expected. Mankind has gone astray and has trampled underfoot the gifts which were given it. There is no order in anything. Even in the highest positions, it is Satan who governs and decides how affairs are to be conducted. He will even know how to find his way to the highest positions in the Church. He will succeed in sowing confusion in the minds of the great scientists who invent arms, with which half of humanity can be destroyed in a few minutes. If mankind does not refrain from wrongdoing and be converted, I shall be forced to let fall my Son's arm. If those at the top, in the world and in the Church, do not oppose these ways, it is I who shall do so, and I shall pray God my Father to visit His justice on mankind.

'There will also come a time of the hardest trials for the Church. Cardinals will be against cardinals, and bishops against bishops. Satan will put himself in their midst. In Rome, also, there will be big changes. What is rotten will fall, and what will fall must not be maintained. The Church will be darkened and the world plunged into confusion.

'God will punish men still more powerfully and harshly than He did by means of the Flood, and the great and powerful will perish just as much as the small and the weak.

The greatest World War will happen in the second half of the twentieth century. Then fire and smoke will fall from the sky, and the waters of the oceans will be turned to steam, hurling their foam towards the sky; and all that is standing will be cast down. Millions and millions of men will lose their lives from one hour to the next, and those who remain living will envy those who are dead. There will be tribulation as far as the eye can see, and misery all over the earth and desolation in every country.

The time is continually approaching, the abyss is growing wider, and there is no end in sight. The good will die with the wicked, the big with the small, the princes of the Church with their faithful, and the sovereigns of the world with their subjects. Satan's henchmen will then be the only sovereigns on earth.

'This will be a time which neither king nor emperor, cardinal nor bishop expects, but it will come, nevertheless, in accordance with my Father's plan to punish and take vengeance. Later, however, when those who survive all this are still alive, God and His glory will once more be invoked, and He will once more be served as He was, not so long ago, when the world had not yet become corrupted.

'I call on all true imitators of my Son, Jesus Christ, all true Christians and apostles of the latter days! The time of times is coming and the end of everything, if mankind is not converted, and if this conversion does not come from above, from the leaders of the world and the leaders of the Church. But woe! Woe if this conversion does not come about, and if all remains as it is, nay, if all becomes even worse!

Go, my child, and proclaim this! I shall always remain by your side to help you.'"

Nothing in this text is either true or authentic: the staggering claim that the text was communicated by the Pope to the heads of state; the historical errors it contains; the literary structure, so different from that employed in Lucia's authentic writings; or the very ideas expressed, so absolutely foreign to those of Sister Lucia. The text is a lamentable copy of the so-called "Secret of La Salette," but even more distorted, exaggerated and falsified.

Thus we see how a series of spurious texts, pandering to unhealthy curiosity and perhaps even with a perverse intention of throwing discredit on Fatima, have sought to take the place of the true text, which remains unpublished. It must be repeated and emphasized that Sister Lucia has never spoken to anyone about the Secret; nor has the Pope, up to the present, judged it opportune to make it known, or to allow it to be made known, to the faithful. Cardinal Ottaviani made this very clear when he said:

Sister Lucia has not spoken. Lucia has kept the Secret. No matter what efforts have been made to persuade her to speak, she has not spoken. Yes, indeed, "Secrets of Fatima" attributed to her are being widely circulated. *Do not believe them!* Lucia has not spoken. She has kept the Secret....In this Lucia has been truly exemplary; she has not spoken. Do not believe those who say they have heard this or that, from Lucia. I, who have had the grace and the gift to read the text of the Secret, I can say that all that is rumored about it is sheer fantasy. You can be certain that the true Secret is guarded in such a manner that no one has set eyes upon it.

The Diocese of Coimbra has also clarified the matter:

The diocesan chancery of Coimbra is authorized to state that Sister Lucia, having said up to the present what she understood should be said on the subject of Fatima, and which is to be found in the various books on Fatima which have been published, has herself, at least from February, 1955 until now, said nothing further, and has therefore never authorized anyone to present to the public anything whatever on the subject of Fatima which claims to be attributed to her.

The present Chapel of the Apparitions at Fatima,
on the spot where Our Lady stood

Conclusion

WE HAVE TRIED IN THESE PAGES TO SHED SOME LIGHT FOR our readers on the Secret of Fatima. We hope that this book will strengthen belief in the apparitions of Our Lady of Fatima and lead those who read it to recognize what constitutes Fatima's essential message: penance, prayer and the intercession of the Immaculate Heart of Mary.

As the Bishop of Marseilles has stated:

> There are far too many people who let themselves be "tossed one way and another and carried along by every wind of doctrine." (Eph. 4, 14). This is a well-known phenomenon. It answers to the double need of personal security and of denouncing those who may be regarded as sources of disturbance. The atmosphere of stress in which we live engenders every possible kind of credulity. People delight in reading heavenly messages which speak of punishments for the bad shepherds of the flock, whether they be bishops or Pope.

All of these pseudo-revelations develop an eschatology of calamity. They unite the attaining of salvation with optional and even suspect devotions; they extol a spirituality which advocates a separation of faith from life and even from the Church and the world.

We can understand the prudence of the Church when it is confronted with private revelations; its rigor and its hesitancy in recognizing some of them; its discretion in determining their character in regard to Revelation, the Word of God lived and celebrated in the Church. Neither the number nor the fervor of the people who accept these revelations is the criterion for their veracity, but solely the judgment of the Pope and the bishops. What is more, we must know that the Church never imposes an apparition as an article of Faith, but contents itself with pronouncing on the content of the message.

First of all, then, educate your Catholic Faith. As the Apostle St. Peter tells us:

Besides, we possess the prophetic message as something altogether reliable. Keep your attention closely fixed on it, as you would on a lamp shining in a dark place until the first streaks of dawn appear and the morning star rises in your hearts. First you must understand this: there is no prophecy contained in Scripture which is a personal interpretation. Prophecy has never been put forward by man's willing it. It is rather that men impelled by the Holy Spirit have spoken under God's influence. (2 Peter 1:19-21).

This applies also to your belief in Fatima, where God's Holy Spirit has been poured out abundantly. What benefit is there in being anxious about the unpublished third part of the Secret, if we still do not take to heart our own conversion and penance and a true and authentic devotion to the Virgin Mary? This alone will prepare us to welcome the disclosure of this unpublished text. We quote once again the Bishop of Leiria: "I am deeply concerned at seeing that people consider the principal part of the Secret to be that which is to be made known in 1960, whereas the most important part is what everyone already knows."

We must not let ourselves be carried away by strange fears about future punishments supposedly contained in the unpublished part of the Secret, and which are no message at all, but merely threatening prophecies. It is much more important to give a true response to what we already know of the message to Fatima.

Fatima today from the air
[*The Basilica is at left and the Chapel of the Apparitions at lower center*]

Epilogue

The English edition of this book is being published in 1979, the fiftieth anniversary of Our Lady's appearance to Sister Lucia at the convent of the Sisters of St. Dorothy at Tuy in Spain.

On June 13, 1929 Our Lady said to Sister Lucia, "God asks the Holy Father, in union with all the bishops of the world, to make the consecration of Russia to my Immaculate Heart, promising to save it by this means." She had said at Fatima in 1917 that when this is done (and presumably not before), Russia will be converted and there will be a period of peace in the world.

Pope Pius XII consecrated the world to the Immaculate Heart of Mary in 1942 and Russia to the Immaculate Heart in 1952, and Pope Paul VI repeated the consecrations on November 21, 1964 in the presence of the fathers of Vatican Council II. Still, as

Father Alonso makes clear in this book, the consecration of Russia has not yet been made *in the way* Our Lady requested fifty years ago.

It is said that the present Holy Father, John Paul II, while still a bishop, was one of those who signed a petition requesting the Pope to carry out Our Lady's wishes. Now that he himself has become the Vicar of Christ, perhaps *he* will consecrate Russia to the Immaculate Heart of Mary in union with all the bishops of the world. This anniversary year certainly seems an appropriate time, and we earnestly recommend such an intention to the prayers and petitions of those who read this book.

The Publishers

OTHER RAVENGATE BOOKS

FATIMA
by Lucy Herself

Over 150,000 copies sold in U.S.

FATIMA FROM THE BEGINNING
by John De Marchi

VIRGIN WHOLLY MARVELOUS
Praises of Our Lady by the Popes, Councils, Saints, and Doctors of the Church
Edited by Peter Brookby

SAINT SHARBEL, Mystic of the East
by Claire M. Benedict

MOTHER SETON, St. Elizabeth of New York
by Leonard Feeney

Ravengate Press * Box 103 * Cambridge, Massachusetts 02238